MAGIC! 2

Teacher's Guide

EUROPEAN LANGUAGE INSTITUTE

P.O. Box 6 - Recanati - Italy
Tel. 071/750701 - Telefax 071/977851

Printed in Italy by Tecnostampa s.r.l.

ISBN **88 - 8148 - 047 - 6**

I. ENGLISH IN PRIMARY SCHOOLS

The teaching of English in primary schools is part of a child's general cultural education. The role of primary education is to promote the acquisition of various types of language with a view to the harmonious development of a child's personality and ability. You are, therefore, invited to overcome the pragmatic aspect of different subjects in order to encourage intelligent comprehension and criticism by the children.
The method of teaching should favour the understanding and appreciation of cultural and linguistic differences and the learning process should be both intellectually stimulating and creative. Stimulating the curiosity and imagination of your pupils must be considered a highly educational purpose. In this way, the children will really enjoy themselves and will relate what they are learning to their own world.
Language learning was once limited to the acquisition of one's own mother tongue. Nowadays, however, a complete linguistic education is seen in terms of comparisons with a foreign language. Making young people aware that other languages and different cultures exist is, without doubt, the best way to prepare them for the multiethnic society of the next century. With this in mind, it is important to promote a "positive attitude" in our children which will act as a catalyst in language acquisition right from the start. Therefore, the activities you propose must be suitable for your pupils' age and ability.

I.A. THE VALUE OF EARLY LEARNING

It is clear that the stage at which and the way in which a foreign language is introduced must be suitable for your pupils. Numerous studies have demonstrated the benefit of learning a foreign language at an early age as it encourages:
a) the development of the logical-deductive processes, useful for all subjects, especially those requiring logical-mathematical skills;
b) greater awareness of one's own mother tongue;
c) greater aptitude for other foreign languages.
In addition, at a pre-school age children show greater mental and phonatory elasticity which gradually diminishes as one gets older to make way for other abilities. The phonatory apparatus is still extremely supple and, therefore, it is easier to produce any type of sound. Children do not have the inhibitions of an adult in making new or strange sounds, and if a child is sufficiently stimulated he/she will never tire of repeating the same thing until the results are almost perfect.
During the first few years of primary school, children become aware of the fact that numerous ways of comunicating exist. The teaching of the various "languages" on the syllabus is concerned with achieving this awareness. A foreign language, therefore, becomes one of the many means that a child can use to express himself or to communicate in different contexts ranging from imaginary ones to situations that are closer to our daily lives. In this way, a child can begin to appreciate the functional value of learning a foreign language.

I.B LEARNING ABOUT INTERNATIONAL CO-OPERATION

It is important not to forget, however, that the fundamental aim of teaching a foreign language at primary level must not consist in early linguistic "training", but rather in a linguistic, psychological and cultural preparation which will be examined more closely at a later stage. The approach to a foreign language at an early age must stress the importance of adopting a spirit of understanding and international cooperation. For a child, contact with a language and a different culture fosters social awareness, understanding and respect, not only for different ways of life, but also for different points of view and contrasting opinions. In this way a child may discover that diversity is above all a source of wealth for all and not a reason for marginalization. Thus we hope that primary schools, thanks to early cultural integration, will encourage the spirit of peace.

I.C. GENERAL AIMS

The general aims of English language teaching are the following:

a) to enrich cognitive development by providing another way to organize knowledge;
b) to enable a child to communicate with other children in another language;
c) to prepare the pupil, by means of language learning, to understand other cultures and other peoples;
d) to develop tolerance and respect towards those cultural aspects of the English-speaking world which differ from one's own;
e) to learn vocabulary by observing and using the most common Anglicisms;
f) to compare fundamental structures used in L1 and L2;
g) to improve a child's ability to analyse and synthesize.

I.D. COMMUNICATIVE-LINGUISTIC AIMS

From an initial oral approach, on the basis of "natural learning", all four language skills (listening, speaking, reading and writing) are developed and consolidated by work on pronunciation, vocabulary and grammatical structures.

Listening is encouraged thanks to the wide use of situational dialogues, songs and nursery rhymes which favour the recognition and understanding of the language and stimulate oral practice.

Simple conversations based on topics of interest for a child (school, colours, animals, numbers, the house, the family, etc.)are proposed in order to develop oral competence in everyday situations (greetings, identifying objects etc.).

Reading is encouraged through simple, but interesting texts with clear illustrations.

The writing skill must be introduced gradually. For this reason, writing is initially only stimulated and used to complete short texts or in games with simple words or phrases.

As far as the grammatical aspect is concerned, the children must be taught to recognize certain structures without specific analysis or terminology. At this stage, it is sufficient to introduce some grammatical structures in appropriate contexts, but without insisting too much. In this way, a child will begin to realise that structures which are different from those of his mother tongue exist. Therefore, grammar is seen as reconstruction and gradual discovery, not as the mechanical learning of models.

More methodical work and more detailed examination of grammatical structures will take place at a later stage. Thus, when studying the language at secondary school the pupils will benefit from the fact that they have already acquired considerable linguistic awareness.

With regard to vocabulary, both oral and written consolidation exercises in the form of games are suggested. In addition, the language used must be introduced progressively, based on a spiral approach which requires the use and comprehension of language forms previously presented.

I.E. PARALINGUISTIC AIMS

A foreign language, as a new means of

expression, stimulates a child's creativity and imagination because it leads to the discovery of a "new world".

It is a well-known fact that children learn thanks to their great sense of curiosity. Likewise for English, their curiosity should be stimulated with the use of games, practical activities, mimed songs and nursery rhymes, role-play and scenes to act out. In this way the children will perceive the immediate use of this new language in either real or imaginary contexts. Its relationship with other subjects becomes evident so that English is not considered an isolated subject.

The English lesson arouses interest if it is presented as a "magic" moment, during which everybody uses a "secret code" to express themselves. Thus, the children will feel involved in this "mysterious" experience and gradually they will feel proud of the fact that they can deal with this "secret code". Besides, the foreign language teacher also helps to:

a) encourage not only logical development, but also attention, concentration and memory;

b) favour socialization and collaboration among classmates;

c) develop manual skills and movement.

II. METHODOLOGY

II.A. THE COMMUNICATIVE APPROACH THROUGH GAMES

This "approach" can be defined as a communicative approach through games.

It is an intelligent approach to a foreign language and culture without using rigid methods. It encourages a positive attitude towards the language which in turn leads to communicative competence.

Children are attracted by games and enjoyable activities.

During the sixteenth and seventeenth centuries, with the beginning of modern educational theory, games (in every sense of the word) were greatly valued because children could both learn and actively exercise their ability, language and emotions. Obviously the games we propose are educational with language learning as their aim. These games have been specially studied to arouse enthusiasm and the desire to learn this "secret code". The purpose of the approach through games is to foster the passion for language learning.

At the same time, this approach is also communicative in the sense that the language is presented as a code for communication right from the start. In this way global communicative activities are suggested and not isolated phrases or words. The children will then have a chance to put into practice what they have been learning during the lesson thanks to the games and activities you propose.

This approach is also based on the "multisensorial" learning approach to a foreign language.

II.B. "NATURAL" LEARNING

By "natural" learning we mean the development of linguistic ability in a similar way to that which enables us to learn our own mother tongue.

During the first few months of life a child hears adults speaking and from this he will develop the ability to associate sounds to objects or functions.

Only at the age of 5 or 6 will he come into contact with reading and writing, and therefore with grammar and its terminology.

So, taking this process as a model, recent teaching studies recommend, when teaching children a foreign language, an approach which initially stimulates mainly oral skills, stressing pronunciation and the communicative function, and then moving on to a consolidation phase which stimulates also the reading and writing skills.

With regard to grammar, it is advisable not to introduce specific grammatical topics or language, as this might initiate comparisons between L2 and L1.

Obviously, you must try to create an atmosphere of "full immersion in the language" which means speaking in English as much as possible and creating "an English atmosphere" which will favour learning. However, this does not prevent you from explaining an activity or a particular fact in L1 at some stage during the lesson. This must not be considered an obstacle, as it is actually a useful way to involve the children and to encourage them. It is important to then return to L2 with a fixed expression (for example, "Ready?" or "Let's play a game") to make it clear that everybody must start speaking only in English. During the first few lessons it is also a good idea to teach useful expressions used in class (for example, how to ask to leave the classroom or to go to the toilet, to ask how you say something in English etc.). This shows the pupils that English has a concrete use and helps them to feel at ease in expressing themselves in English.

II.C MULTISENSORY LEARNING

The communicative approach through games is further supported by the awareness that efficient teaching needs to call on all the sensory perceptions in order to involve children completely in the learning process.

For learning to take place, both cerebral hemispheres have to work together harmoniously. Since each hemisphere develops different abilities, it is necessary to involve not only the specifically linguistic capabilities, which are found in the left hemisphere, but also the creative and perceptive capabilities of the right hemisphere.

Normally the left hemisphere dominates logical thought, phonetics, reading and writing while the right one is responsible for spacial-temporal relationships, models and forms, mathematical calculations, the perception of colour, musical aptitude, feelings and emotions. Bearing this in mind the teaching of English uses the three principal senses during the learning process. This means using visual, hearing and practical (movement, touch, concrete experience) activities to elicit the use of all the sensorial dimensions by the children.

Multisensorial learning involves various activities which favour the "Total Physical Response" through games. Attractive, colourful pictures are an ideal way to introduce words without having to translate and, at the same time, guarantee a greater ability to memorize as the visual aid helps one remember. Songs and nursery rhymes help the pupils overcome inhibitions and shyness, above all if they sing or recite as a group.

Songs also help with the pronunciation of unusual sounds as well as the repetition of vocabulary and structures. Role play, games involving movement and practical activities help learning thanks to concrete experience.

Such an approach takes into account the needs of a varied group, as children from the age of 7 or 8 learn in the way that suits them best. Therefore, multisensory learning helps pupils to understand better and to learn in a more efficient and motivating way.

II.D. TEACHING CHILDREN HOW TO STUDY

Psychologists and sociologists have recently stressed the importance of direct student involvement in the learning process.

Only in this way will the learner feel directly stimulated and learn how to study and to evaluate his progress: he will learn how to learn.

With this in mind, you must clarify the

purpose and meaning of each exercise or lesson, making sure that the pupils understand what they have to do and why. At the same time, you must encourage the pupils to have confidence in their ability and to develop self-appraisal, creating a serene atmosphere in which mistakes are not a cause of embarrassment and the pupils' progress is appreciated and rewarded.
So you have to provide all the necessary stimuli for efficient learning and encourage the students to check themselves by involving them in correcting work in class.

II.E MIMING AND GESTURES
In order to create "an English atmosphere" in class to offer students full immersion in thc language, it is useful to know how to fully exploit mime and gestures, providing each word or structure with an explanatory gesture. Pupils can be asked to repeat the same movement so that they can memorize the meaning with a concrete experience which calls on the "Total Physical Response".

III. PRESENTATION OF THE COURSE

III. A. MAGIC!
It is a three-level course for primary school children who are learning English for the first time. The main aim is for them to enjoy themselves as they learn. The course is based on an exciting story, which links the three volumes, and also includes songs, nursery rhymes and games. In this way, the children will be stimulated to learn English, to express themselves and communicate in L2 and to find out about the English-speaking world.
The entire course follows the adventures of David and Helen, two English twins, and their dog Floppy. One day they meet Peter Pan and this meeting introduces imaginary themes into the story. Besides being able to fly, Peter can do other "magic tricks" such as changing the colour of things and animals and making someone invisible. But Peter's most exciting trick is making the twins and Floppy able to fly. This will lead them all to new extraordinary adventures.
The choice of Peter Pan as the principal character in the story fulfils an important duty, by teaching us to accept others for what they are. Peter is a boy with both good and bad qualities: he occasionally monopolizes the situation, at times he is too exuberant as he dominates the twins' life and turns it upside down. David and Helen, however, accept him for what he is and introduce him to their group of friends. Accepting others for what they are, therefore, is presented as an important value, above all in our increasingly multi-ethnic society.
The two twins show Peter Pan around their town, they introduce him to their friends and their family, they offer him their food and show him the things they like doing. But, just when they have become good friends a message from Neverland arrives: Peter has to go back. So, at the end of the first course book Peter returns to Neverland taking the two twins and their dog with him.
The adventures in the second volume continue on the imaginary island of Neverland in which two new characters, Hook and Smythe, appear. In the third course book the characters go on a trip around the world to solve the mystery surrounding the disappearance of Tinker Bell.
Particular attention has been paid to aspects and traditions of the English-speaking world in both illustrations and the story.
The course can also be linked with other subjects such as geography, science and mathematics.

III.B. TEACHING MATERIALS
For each level, a textbook is provided for

the student and a guide, two cassettes and a set of posters for the teacher.

In the **student's book,** new words, structures and functions are introduced in each unit. The presentation of new language proceeds gradually and is based on a spiral approach which requires the use and understanding of language forms previously introduced. In this way, numerous songs, nursery rhymes and games are inserted to practice new language and stress correct pronunciation. The story also gives you the chance to involve areas of study from other subjects. The exercises, which are mainly based on games, supply material for the consolidation phase either in class or at home and enable the pupils to use the language they have learnt in an enjoyable way.

The **student's audiocassette** has all the nursery rhymes and songs introduced in the textbook which means that the pupils can listen on their own to both the words and the music.

The **teacher's guide**, available for each level, suggests the best way to use the book with the aim of motivating the children and stimulating the four specific skills: listening, speaking, reading and writing. The guide also offers a wide variety of ideas and suggestions for additional games suitable for children of this age. These suggestions have already been tried out with sample classes of pupils learning English at a young age.

Part of the guide has been dedicated to the presentation, consolidation and revision of the alphabet with activities, songs and graded games. The alphabet has not been presented in the textbook in order to give you complete freedom in deciding when and if to deal with the subject.

After a Welcome Unit based on the revision of the structures introduced during the previous academic year, 10 units each divided into 3 lessons follow. After the fifth and tenth units there is a section entirely dedicated to revision and consolidation activities, followed by a test which can be photocopied. Some notes for the teacher are also included. Only Unit 11, in the first volume which is about a trip to Great Britain, is divided into 8 lessons. In the second course book, Unit 11, after an introductory section, presents six traditional European stories and legends. In all three volumes, Unit 12 concludes the story in one lesson, and hints at new adventures to follow.

The teacher's cassette provides the correct pronunciation and intonation for the dialogues, listening comprehensions, songs and rhymes in the book. The variety of activities which can be carried out using the tape favour the development of the speaking and listening skills, and it is very useful if you want to practise difficult sounds in an amusing way.

The **set of posters** included with each guide supply visual aids that are ready for use. The ***Alphabet Poster*** provides a clear illustration of the capital letters, of the sounds expressed with the international phonetic alphabet, of words starting with small letters and their relative pictures. The poster offers a precise reference point for numerous graded activities presented in the appropriate section of the guide regarding the presentation, consolidation and revision of the alphabet. The phonetic transcription of the sounds facilitates the learning of the alphabet and it provides a visual approach to the symbols that the children will come across when they consult a bilingual dictionary.

The Magic Wand Poster can be used to illustrate the pupils' results and progress in the individual tests and in the work done at home and at school during class activities.

III.C. THE FOUR SKILLS

Since the development of the four skills has been set as a specific linguistic purpose, all

the basic activities have been formulated with this in mind.
Regarding the **listening skill**, the pupils are encouraged to guess the meaning of what is said on the basis of the context so that they can check their ideas and get a psychological incentive out of it. Children generally make the most out of mimes, gestures, accents and tones of voice used to make oneself understood.
The listening activities are highlighted with the following titles: *close your eyes and listen* during which the children must concentrate on the sounds and then say which sound struck them most because it is unusual, nice, musical etc...; *look and listen, listen and repeat/ mime/ point/ answer/ think/ speak/ write/ find/ check/ move/ sing/ match/ colour/ draw/ number*; while *time for playback* provides an ideal way to move on to the speaking skill.
The oral activities in *Magic! 1* get the children involved first in *choral practice role-play*, then in *group practice role-play* and only at a later stage after a number of repetitions, in *individual practice role-play* and *act it out*.
In the other volumes, besides acting out the dialogues, we propose guided *role-play* which gradually lead on to freer *role-play,* thereby permitting the children to express themselves with a certain amount of autonomy.
The ability to read will be stimulated by means of discrimination exercises (*read and find out, read and circle*), completion (*read and match, read and complete*) and various types of activities such as *read and do, read and answer, read and colour.*
In *Magic! 2* the pupils will be asked to read simplified short stories and to do various activities associated with the texts: *pre-reading, while-reading* (such as *fill in the gap, play a role in the narration*) and *after-reading* (such as *underline the words you recognise, let's play with words, reconstructing the text*).
Magic! 3 offers simple descriptive texts about the wonders of the anglo-saxon world.
Writing has long been relegated to second place when teaching children a foreign language, but recent studies have re-evaluated its importance because it gradually encourages creative writing on the basis of given models such as nursery rhymes that the children can modify as they wish according to their language level. Specific written exercises are indicated with *copy, match, complete, write, break the code and find the message.*

III.D. TEACHING NOTES
Given that each teacher has a diverse group of children each with different needs, it is clear that, more often than not, only when you are in the classroom with the children will you be able to appreciate the efficiency of the teaching suggestions and activities. On occasions, you might have to change your lesson plans at the last moment because something unexpected comes up.
Nevertheless, this book is an articulated guide, rich in suggestions and ideas that you can choose to adopt or modify according to your needs. It should take you three lessons to cover one unit of the textbook, apart from Unit 11 in volumes 1 and 2 which is spread over a number of lessons.
One conclusive lesson should be dedicated to Unit 12. Each lesson follows a regular plan so that the pupils can learn to recognize the various phases of the lesson and to collaborate during them. Generally the plan is as follows:
- ***warm-up or revision*** to start the lesson off in a relaxing way with an interesting activity which provides a break from the previous lesson;
- ***checking homework*** to involve the pupils in the correction of homework either in pairs or all together;
- ***presentation*** to introduce a dialogue or new vocabulary and structures often through listening activities;

- ***practice*** during which the children practise both structures and pronunciation by means of games or other amusing activities;
- ***consolidation*** using various types of activities aimed at revising and consolidating what has already been learnt;
- ***revision*** to revise vocabulary or structures that the pupils have learnt in previous units.
- *the* ***revision activities*** every five lessons offer further consolidation by means of specific games to practise structures and vocabulary used in different communicative situations.

For further detail turn to the relevant stage in the guide for each unit.

The evaluation of each child's effort and results must be judged in relation to the individual's ability. You should therefore try to find the appropriate moment to praise even the weaker elements thereby stimulating them to apply themselves to the full. The course recommends the use of a poster with a graded magic wand, *The Magic Wand Poster*, which is included with the guide.

The cards with the children's names are placed in the notches. These cards will be moved up a notch according to your appraisal of each child (from participation in games or activities, to homework, results of tests in class etc..).

The position of the cards will show the children the level of the "magical skill" they have acquired.

In this way, the pupils will be able to see directly how much progress they are making and they will be motivated to try to possess more of that "magic", which is in reality the English language, represented by the magic wand. The children are bound to be enthusiastic about this method of evaluation because of its magical touch and its competitive connotations which you must handle delicately. At the end of the year, all the pupils should reach the top of the wand.

III.E. TESTS

Each revision and consolidation phase concludes with a test in class, which will take one lesson. It is important to make the children understand that English is just like any other subject on the syllabus, and therefore, the same amount of effort must be dedicated to it. At the same time, the test should be presented as a way to check what the pupils have learnt, but above all as another enjoyable challenge for them.

Thanks to this emphasis, the children will learn to face tests calmly and in this way they will do the best they can.

III.F. INDIVIDUAL AND TEAM GAMES

With regard to games, it is important to establish some norms with an educational purpose.

Competitiveness stimulates learning, but you must make sure that the atmosphere in the class doesn't become tense. It is advisable, therefore, that when selecting teams you should try to make them as homogeneous as possible while making sure that the formations seem quite casual.

This favours team spirit and makes children of different levels collaborate on equal ground. Criteria for the choice of groups could be: date of birth, the children's initials, or the number of letters that make up their names or anything else you are able to evaluate purposely.

The losers, could be made to do some amusing forfeits which serve to brush up old and new vocabulary (for example repeat a word that is difficult to pronounce a certain number of times, find one or more words on a poster or on a page of the textbook within a time limit, do particular actions etc...). The pupils could actually decide for themselves what forfeit they have to do before starting the game.

The periodic tests in class are articulated games testing specific abilities which enable

the pupils, according to their results, to possess more "magic" of the English language.
The pupils' progress, each time, will be measured on the Magic Wand Poster by moving the names up a notch or two.
To make sure the activities and games proceed correctly, you can't avoid giving explanations in L1. Choose an opening phrase which will act as a signal for the children to get ready to play a particular game (eg. *Let's sing a song, Let's play bingo, Let's play the game* etc..) and to warn them that from that moment on they can only speak English. If they want to revert back to L1, the students have to ask *Can I speak (mother tongue)?* but not more than a few times during the course of the game.
If the pupils do not show interest in a particular game, then you should be ready to interrupt it and suggest an alternative activity. If the children are bored or lose interest, the game is no longer productive. For this reason, the activities must proceed rapidly, but in an orderly fashion, so that an element of surprise and competition is maintained. The course offers numerous examples of games and activities which have been experimented in trial classes.

III.G. SONGS, NURSERY RHYMES AND POEMS

An oral approach is the best way to handle the songs, nursery rhymes and poems. This means that the children should first learn the correct pronunciation and, at a later stage, see the written text. So, the pupils should listen to the song/nursery rhyme/poem initially with their eyes closed, in order to concentrate on the listening skill.
The children listen to the cassette a few more times so that they can concentrate on the pronunciation and recognize the structures or words that they have already come across. To make the last few minutes of the lesson a relaxing and enjoyable moment, you could involve the children actively with this activity.
To learn the song/nursery rhyme/poem correctly it is wise to teach all the words, otherwise the activity might lose spontaneity. Let the children participate actively during the miming stage and let them join in vocally when they feel ready to do so. It is important to stimulate the pupils adequately and to do so you could use the "stress-timing" technique making them keep time with the song/nursery rhyme/poem. Ask them to snap their fingers, tap their knees or clap to the rhythm of the text.
All the songs/nursery rhymes/poems can be mimed which will help the children understand the meaning.
In addition, to ensure that repetition is always a profitable and never a boring activity, you could establish different ways to repeat each time, for example; you could use the playback method, change the speed (slowly/quickly) or divide the children into different groups, each with a part to sing or recite.
At this stage, the children will have already learnt the pronunciation and they will be prepared to look at the words, which they should understand, having worked out their meaning thanks to the miming activity.
The pupils can now see the written text and they will undoubtedly notice the difference between the written word and the pronunciation, but with minor risk of interference.
As an additional creative writing activity you could ask the children to rewrite the song by changing a few words as they wish. This stage is also useful as a means of revising and consolidating pronunciation and the vocabulary that has been learnt. By collecting both the original and reinvented versions of the songs/nursery rhymes/poems in a "class song-book" you will have a reference book at hand to consult when you want to choose a song to sing or a rhyme to recite.

III.H. PRACTICAL ACTIVITIES

The practical activities can also be exploited linguistically, while something concrete is being produced. In fact, the children will find it very easy to associate the word with its meaning since they have to use the objects that are named. It is important to introduce words clarifying their meaning immediately; then the children will get used to using only English expressions during the practical activities in class.

These activities can be very varied: from making a poster to colouring in a page of the textbook.

The language used during these activities will become part of the "English in the classroom". During the course the pupils may be asked to do a *project* which will be illustrated on a poster and can then be used as a visual aid for a variety of activities.

It is important that the children realise that, through these practical activities, they are learning to express themselves in a foreign language.

IV. ENGLISH IN THE CLASSROOM

We suggest you use English in class as much as possible, so that the children can practise using the language directly in real situations. It is advisable to introduce simple expressions from the first lesson and gradually add new ones.
The following list gives a few expressions that are easy to understand if accompanied by mimes and gestures, and they will become part of the students' passive vocabulary.

To greet people:
Hello!
Good morning!
Good afternoon!

To introduce the lesson:
How are you? I'm fine, thank you. And you?
Are you ready?
Who's absent today?
Sit down.
Be quiet.
Let's start the lesson.
What's the date?
What's the weather like today?
What's your name? My name is ...
How old are you? I'm ...
This is ...

To attract attention:
Listen!
Pay attention!
Remember!
Look at me!

To give instructions:
Write!
Draw!
Copy!
Complete!
Work in pairs!
Ask (him/her)!
Speak up, please!
Take your crayons/pencil/pen/book...
Put your exercise book on the desk.
Open your book at page ...
Repeat after me/with me/all together.
Don't repeat!
Can you repeat?
Pardon?
Try again.
Match!
Show me ...
Point to ...
Close your book/exercise book.
Look at page ...
Look at this picture!
Turn the page.
Colour!
Cut...

To conclude the lesson:
The lesson is over.
Put away your book/exercise book.
Finish the exercise at home.
This is your homework.
Complete this.
Goodbye!
See you next lesson.
Goodbye boys and girls/children!
Bye bye! / Have a nice weekend!

To introduce songs, rhymes or poems:
Close your eyes and listen.
Listen to this tune/song/rhyme.
Sing!
Let's sing together!
Sing again!
Group one sings/says the first part.
Group two sings/says the second part.

To play:
Let's play a game!
Right.
We are going to play a game!
Look!
Listen, be quiet!
This game is called ...
Give out ... please!

Look. I've got ...
Take your ...
Here you are!
Move your chairs/desks.
Put your.... over there, please.
Look at me. This is an example.
I want (two) volunteers, please.
Come here!
Come out/to the front of the class!
Stand in a line please!
Two by two, please.
Get into groups of ...
In groups of ...
Make a circle!
You go with ...
It's your turn!
Good!
That's right!
OK!
Correct!
Wrong!
Out!
You're out!
Wait a moment!
Guess ...
Stop the game!
The game is over!
One point for ...
(Group 1) is the winner!

In order to get the children to communicate in English, it is important that, right from the first lesson, they learn to use a certain number of useful phrases, for example:
Can I go out/to the toilet?
Can I clean the board?
Can I put the book away?
Can you repeat, please?
Can I have a .....please?
How do you say it in English/(mother tongue)?
What does it mean, please?
I don't understand.

To encourage the children to use these expressions, you could prepare some "speech bubbles" containing these useful expressions and pin them on the wall to help the pupils learn them.

Alphabet

Note

The alphabet has deliberately not been introduced in the textbook so that you can decide whether and when to handle the subject.
The ABC Poster provided may act as the starting point for a series of graded activities to introduce, consolidate and revise the alphabet.
To make some of the activities more effective, we advise you to hang up the poster at a suitable height for your students.
In the following activities the use of particular vocabulary and grammatical structures is highlighted.

The A-B-C Poster

The ability to pronounce and understand the English alphabet should not be undervalued.
When asking for or supplying precise information such as a name, a surname, an address etc. knowledge of the alphabet is extremely useful.
Even though it is not a main aim of English language learning in primary schools, the alphabet is suggested through graded activities and in association with many structures.
A phonetic transcription has been included on the A-B-C Poster because it facilitates the learning of the alphabet and it provides the pupils with a visual approach which they will come across later on when they consult a bilingual dictionary.
Obviously, at this stage, you do not need to go into the matter in great detail.
You might like to simply explain to your pupils that the symbols will help them to remember the "names" of the letters and that learning to recognize and associate them with particular sounds will make the pronunciation of new words easier for them.
In order to clarify the symbol-sound relationship, where possible, you can relate the phonetic sound of some symbols with the corresponding mother-tongue sounds.
Some practical advice: pin up the poster so that the children can easily reach it.

THE ALPHABET: PRESENTATION

The A-B-C Chant

To introduce the English alphabet, say "The A-B-C Chant" and point out the phonetic symbols on the poster.
ABC - DE - FG
HI - JK - LM
NO - PQ
RS - TU
VW - XYZ.

Comparing Alphabets

The children are bound to notice some letters on the A-B-C Poster that do not appear in their alphabet. At this point, you could take the opportunity to compare the two alphabets.
After an oral explanation, ask the pupils to write the following in their exercise books:
- This is our alphabet....
  There are (number) letters.
- This is the English alphabet....
  There are (number) letters.
- The number of different letters is .... .

This activity can be done either in class or at home.
Tell the children to use capital letters and to write in pencil, but not to colour in the letters, as this will be done during a specific activity.
The page with the English alphabet will be used for the *Listen and Touch, Listen and colour, What colour is A?, Listen and Match* and *Find the word* activities.

CONSOLIDATION

Vowel Chant

To help the pupils learn the pronunciation of the vowels, you could use the following *chant*:

I -A - E - O - U
I'd like to play with you
I - A - E - U - O
Come on! Let's go!
I - A - U - O - E
Just you and me
I - U - O - E - A
We can play all day
U - O - E - A - I
Good-bye! Good-bye!

You might need to mime or translate the phrases in the chant into L1, if the students have never come across them.
You could also act out the chant. Write the words on the blackboard, then call a child out to the front of the classroom to recite the chant and to mime the actions.
To *I'd like to play with you*, the pupil turns to another member of the class, who then gets up and joins him/her. For the last line, both of them pretend to go out of the room waving good-bye to the rest of the class.
To involve the others while the chant is being dramatized, get them to repeat the vowel sequences.

Listen and Touch

STRUCTURES: *(John) come here, please.*
Now touch (B).
Yes, right.
Wrong. Try again.
Go to your place.

Stand near the A-B-C Poster and ask one pupil to come up and touch the letter you say. Use the above-mentioned structures.
Afterwards, this game could be done by the pupils in pairs as a *Test your friend* activity. One child takes the part of the teacher and asks his/her friend to touch the letter he/she says. When his/her partner touches the right letter, then the children swop parts. Proceed in a chain until all the students have had the chance to be the teacher.

Go and touch

For this game, divide the class into two teams each of which has to stand in a line. As soon as you say: *Go and touch (B)*, the first child in each line has to run towards the A-B-C Poster and touch the letter that has been called out.
The pupil who arrives first and touches the right letter is the winner and his/her team gets two points.
If the first student to arrive doesn't touch the correct letter, then his/her opponent has the chance to see if he/she can select the right letter. If the answer is correct, then his/her team wins one point. The team with the highest score wins the game.

Listen and colour

VOCABULARY: *colours*
STRUCTURES: *Pick up grey.*
Find A - A is grey.
Find H - H is grey.
Find J - J is grey.
Find K - K is grey.
A H J K are grey
A H J K are grey
B C D E G P T V are green.
I Y are white.
F L M N S X Z are red.
Q U W are blue.
O is yellow.
R is orange.

Ask the children to put the following colours on their desks: grey, green, white, red, blue, yellow and orange. Then tell them to open their exercise books at the page with the alphabet (re. "Comparing Alphabets"). Say that they are going to colour the letters according to the instructions given to them.
Before moving on to the next colour, get the pupils to repeat the sequence of letters they have just coloured all together. Tell the children to remember the sound which links the letters and the colour.
When you get to the letter R, point out that no colour has the same sound as this letter, so the choice of "orange" is arbitrary.
This activity provides a suitable lead in to other exercises such as *Look and tell the colour* and *Listen and match*.

Look and tell the colour

VOCABULARY: *Colours*
STRUCTURES: *What colour's A?*

With exercise books open at the page with the English alphabet, the pupils, in pairs, ask what colour the different letters are, using the above-mentioned structure. The children take it in turns to ask the question.

Listen and match

STRUCTURES: *Which are the grey letters?*

Give the colour and the pupils have to remember all the letters of the alphabet associated with it.

The Bingo Chant

Teach the pupils the following chant, which could be useful when introducing any type of *Bingo*:

Let's play BINGO
/bi:/, /ai/, /en/, /dʒi:/, /oʊ/ -
/bi:/, /ai/, /en/, /dʒi:/, /oʊ/ -
Let's play BINGO
Let's play BINGO

The Alphabet Bingo

Before starting the game, the children draw a grid with 9 squares each containing a letter of their choice, in their exercise books. Call out the letters in any order, or ask a pupil to do so. As each letter is read out, write it on a sheet of paper to avoid repetition.
If a child has the letter that has been called out in one of his/her squares, then he/she must put a cross on it. The first person to cross out all the letters and to say "BINGO" is the winner.
Decide whether to let the game go on until all the letters of the alphabet have been called out to allow everyone to complete their grid.
The first child to say "Bingo!", will call out the letters in the following game.

Repeat the last letter and add one

Get the children to stand, or sit in a circle and start the game by saying a letter. For the first round you could start with "A". The pupil on your right has to repeat the letter you have said and add another.
Proceed in this way until someone breaks the chain either because he/she can't remember the letter that follows or because he/she pronounces it incorrectly. If this is the case, the game has to start again, but first the pupil who made the mistake has to do a small forfeit (eg. say 3 words that begin with the letter that broke the chain).
To make the game more difficult, you might like to suggest the following variations:

Repeat the last letter and add two
Repeat the last letter and add three
Repeat all the letters and add one

Colour and find out

VOCABULARY: *Colours and numbers*
STRUCTURE: *Colour B4 black.*
or *B4 is black.*

Get the pupils to prepare a grid with 10 horizontal squares with the letters from A to J, and 10 vertical ones with the numbers from 1 to 10.
The students must colour in the squares according to the instructions you give them (for example; Colour B4 black). At the end, the children compare the grids they have coloured. If anyone has made a mistake, then make them do a small forfeit.
The children can do this activity in pairs.

Have you got a name beginning with ('P')?

STRUCTURE: *Have you got ...?*
Yes, I have. / No, I haven't.

Ask one member of the class: *Have you got a name beginning with ('P')?*
to which the pupil replies either affermatively or negatively.

Variations:
Have you got a name with a ('G') in it?
Who's got a name with a ('G') in it?

Present this activity as a *chant.*
Address the class saying:
Who's got a name with a "G" in it?
Then pointing at one child ask:
Is that you?
If the child has that letter in his/her name, he/she will answer:
Yes, me.
Then say:
Oh, good. Now, who's got a name with a "P" in it? and pointing at another pupil say:
Is that you?
If the pupil has not got a name with a "P", he/she replies:
No, not me.
In this case, ask the same child:
Then who? and he/she says the name of a classmate with that letter in his/her name, for example: *Paul.*

USING THE ALPHABET TO REVISE VOCABULARY

1, 2, 3, touch something beginning with...

Put any letter of the alphabet at the end of the above phrase and the pupils have to touch an object in the classroom that begins with that letter.

1, 2, 3, I can see something beginning with...

Find an object in the room and write its name on a piece of paper.
Each time repeat the phrase:
1, 2, 3, I can see something beginning with...
completing it with the initial letter of the chosen object. The pupils who think they can guess the object put up their hands. The first person to make a correct guess, chooses the object the next time round. Help the pupils say the phrase until they know it off by heart.
If you want to do this activity as a team game, divide the class into two teams and decide on the scoring system, for example: 2 points for whoever guesses the object, 1 for the person that names an object which has the same initial letter, but is not the right one. The members of each team take it in turns to call out a name.
Write the scores relating to each team on the

board. Obviously, the team with the highest score wins the game.
If you want to make the game more complex, tell the pupils to name the objects using the following structures:

Teacher: *1, 2, 3, I can see something beginning with ("P")*
Pupil 1: *Is it a pen?*
Teacher: *No, it isn't.*
Pupil 2: *Is it a pencil?*
Teacher: *Yes, it is.*

During the game the part of the teacher can be taken by the person who guesses the object.

What's in your schoolbag?

VOCABULARY: *objects that can be found in a schoolbag*
STRUCTURES: *list of objects preceded by the indefinite article*
In my ... there is a/an...
or:
In my ... I have got a/an ...
or:
In my ... I can see a/an ...

Draw a picture of a schoolbag on the blackboard with 5 or more letters of the alphabet inside.
Individually or in groups, the pupils write as many words starting with the letters indicated and that could refer to objects found in a child's schoolbag.
The child or group that manages to find the most words within the time limit wins the game. You could also use the same activity to revise other vocabulary by changing the initial picture (for example, a fruit bowl, a shopping bag, a suitcase, a room, a toy box etc.).
To make the game easier, you could let the pupils consult the textbook.

Find the words

Divide the class into small groups and then write a sequence of 10 letters (3 vowels and 7 consonants) on the board. The students copy them down into their exercise books.
The purpose of the game is to find as many words as possible using the given letters within a time limit.
You could give a point for each correct word that is found.
Afterwards, you could suggest the following variation:

Find the longest word

Each pupil has to try to make up the longest word using, only the letters on the board.

FROM THE ALPHABET TO THE SPELLING

A is for (apple)

The A-B-C Poster will also be useful to consolidate or to learn new words.
Indicate the pictures that illustrate the alphabet saying: *A is for apple.*
If the pupils ask why the letter A in *apple* isn't pronounced like its alphabetical sound, explain that all the vowels are slightly irregular and do not always maintain their "name".
For the time being, tell the children to concentrate on remembering the word and its sound.

Spelling from the A-B-C Poster

STRUCTURE: *Can you spell ..., please?*

Ask one member of the class to spell a word chosen from the A-B-C Poster. The pupil will then ask another child to spell another

word and so on round the class.
Alternatively, this activity can be performed in pairs or in small groups.

Crosses

The children draw a grid with 9 squares (3x3) and copy down a word from the A-B-C Poster in each square.
Call out the letters of the alphabet (noting them down to avoid repetition). The pupils have to draw a cross on top of the word that starts with the letter that you have called out. The first person to form a horizontal, vertical or diagonal line is the winner.

Spell and find out

Referring to the A-B-C Poster, call out a word and ask a pupil to spell it. Then ask the children to find new words that begin with the letters that form the word given.
For example: *CAT /si:/, /ei:/, /ti:/*
C is for Cup
A is for Apple
T is for Table
At first, start with the words on the poster, then the pupils can extend the activity to include all the words they know.

Find the hidden word

VOCABULARY: *numbers (from 1 to 26 or from 1 to 100)*
STRUCTURES: *Write ... (list of numbers)*
What's the word?

Referring to the page with the English alphabet in their exercise books, explain to the children that each number corresponds to a letter (1 for A, 2 for B, 3 for C etc..). Write a word in numbers on the blackboard (for example: 3,1,20) which the pupils have to copy down and then decode.
Fix a time limit, and the first child to finish dictates the letters saying:
Number 3 is /si:/, number 1 is /ei:/, number 20 is /ti:/
The word is: CAT.
Later on, you could write a phrase instead of a single word.
In order to practise other numbers, you could ask the pupils to number the letters of the alphabet choosing any number from 1 to 100. Each pupil could say a number for each letter, for example:
A is number 14.
In pairs, each student writes a word or a phrase in numbers on a piece of paper and then passes it to his/her partner who has to find the hidden word or phrase.

Circle and find out

VOCABULARY: *colours*
STRUCTURES: *Take red and circle*
/si:/, /ei:/, /ti:/
Finished.
What word is it?

Get the children to open their textbooks at any page containing words or sentences. Then tell them to take a colour and to circle the letters you say, forming a word that the children must read out, either individually or all together. Change colour each time you start a new word.

What is /pi:/, /i:/, /en/?

Tell the children to copy the spelling of some words (first short ones then longer ones) into their exercise books. Then individual pupils choose a word and spell it. This activity could be done as a competition. Establish the maximum number of words and assign a point for each word spelt correctly.

Eaten!

Divide the class into two teams and give each team a symbol. Then write the first letter of a word on the blackboard followed by a number of dashes (each dash represents a letter).
To simplify the game, you could also give the last letter and mark the vowels in the word with a cross (+).
Beneath the word draw each team's symbol followed by the number of dashes corresponding with the letters in the word.
Then draw a shark with its mouth open. Draw a man on the first dash. The teams take it in turns to call out a letter of the alphabet. If the word has that letter write it above the respective dash. If, to the contrary, the letter does not appear in the word, draw a half-loop from the man which represents a step towards the mouth of the shark. Obviously, the first team to be eaten by the shark loses the game. Conduct the game yourself the first few times.
Afterwards, the pupils can take over. Before starting, get them to write the word on a sheet of paper and the right number of dashes. If the pupils still have difficulty in associating the leters with the sounds, tell them to write the corresponding phonetic symbol from the A-B-C Poster beneath each letter.

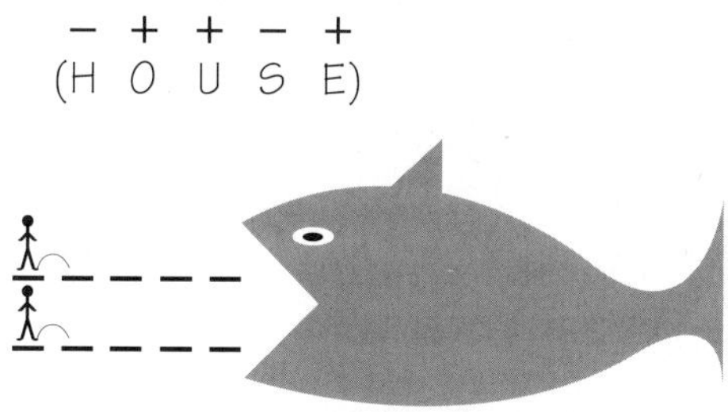

Welcome unit

Lesson 1 pages 4-5

Materials: *Magic 1*; small pieces of paper divided into two groups, one containing questions the other the respective answers (re. II,1 for examples)
Revision of **functions** and **structures** introduced in *Magic 1*
Vocabulary: *Fantastic!, Wonderful!, At last!*

I. PRESENTATION

1. What do you remember?
During the first lesson it is a good idea to do activities which enable the students to remember the basic structures and vocabulary introduced during the previous academic year.
In order to help your pupils, bring a copy of *Magic 1* to the lesson. As you flick through the book remind the class of the dialogues and ask the pupils various questions in L1 so that they can call to mind David and Helen's adventures with Peter Pan. *Unit 12* of *Magic 1* relates to the introductory page of the new course, where the main characters are flying to the island of Neverland.

2. Welcome to Neverland (p. 4-5)
Let the pupils listen to what the characters are saying by playing the cassette. Tell them to look at the island and describe it in L1.

II. REVISION

1. Find your partner
Hand out the small pieces of paper, with the following questions and answers:

- *What's your name?* **My name's David.**
- *How old are you?* **I'm ten.**
- *When's David's birthday?* **It's in February.**
- *Who's Peter Pan?* **He's my friend.**
- *Who's Helen?* **She's David's sister.**
- *Where's Floppy?* **He's in the kennel.**
- *Can I have your pen, please?* **Yes, here you are!**
- *Are you thirsty?* **Yes, I am. Can I have a coke, please?**
- *Do you like fruit?* **No, I don't like fruit.**
- *What is it?* **It's my schoolbag.**
- *What's your favourite animal?* **It's the crocodile.**
- *What's that?* **That's Tower Bridge.**
- *What time is it?* **It's four o'clock.**
- *What colour are your jeans?* **They're blue.**
- *How many pupils are there in your class?* **There are twenty-two.**

After having shuffled the pieces of paper, distribute them randomly and get the pupils to walk around the classroom to find another person with the corresponding question or answer.
As the pairs are formed tell the children to stand in two lines: one with the pupils who have got a question and the other with those who have got an answer.
At the end of the activity, tell the children to read out the contents of their pieces of paper in turns. In this way, you will be able to check both the pairs of questions and answers as well as the pronunciation and intonation.
Once the pupils have read out their sentences, you could ask them to translate the phrase into their mother tongue to check comprehension.

2. A game: Noughts and crosses

This game, which the students should already know as it was introduced in *Magic 1* (U6.L3.IV,3), helps to revise vocabulary and structures in an enjoyable way with the participation of the whole class.
Divide the pupils into two teams and tell them to choose a name for themselves (for example: the tigers/the lions). Then draw a grid with 9 squares (3x3) on the blackboard. Assign each column a colour, *red, pink, blue*; and the rows a number, *one, two, three*. This will help the teams to identify the square in which they wish to place their symbol: a nought or a cross.
Give each team a symbol and tell them to choose a spokesman. Decide who starts the game by doing the *One potato* counting rhyme (ref: *Magic 1*: U4.L3.VI,2).
Ask each team questions such as:
- *Can you name (number) colours / (wild/domestic) animals/fruit/food/rooms/ objects in the classroom/family members?*

to revise vocabulary;
- *What's the English for:* (provide common expressions in your mother tongue and get the students to translate them into Engish) to practice expressions and structures.

You should point out at the beginning of the game that if the pronunciation or intonation is incorrect then the word passes to the other team, which can try to correct the mistake and therefore win the point. Then ask:
Where shall I put the nought/cross?
The spokesman for the team must then indicate where he/she wants you to put his/her symbol saying, for example:
Three-blue.
Then it is the other team's turn to play.
The first team to make a line of noughts or crosses in any direction (horizontal, vertical, diagonal) wins the game.

3. Chant the verb to be

Get the pupils to position themselves as in

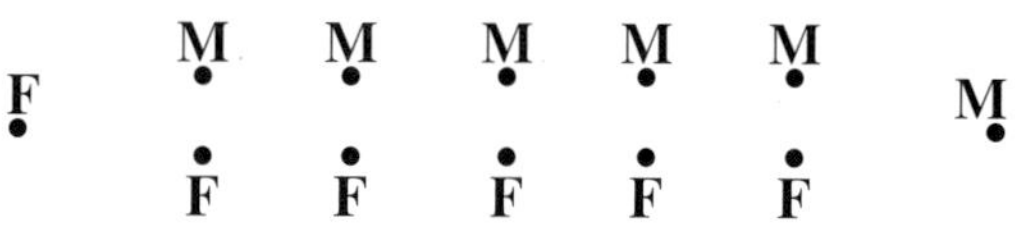

the diagram:
To revise the verb *to be* introduce the following chant:

I am, I am, I am, I am
(each child points to himself/herself)
You are, you are, you are, you are
(each child points at the classmate opposite him/her)
He is, he is
(point at the boy on one side)
She is, she is
(point at the girl on one side)
We are
(a big gesture to indicate your group)
You are
(a big gesture to indicate the group opposite)
They are
(point at the children on the other side)
Once the chant has been repeated without any mistakes, it can be used to revise the interrogative and negative forms of the verb to be.

III. HOMEWORK

Tell the children to bring *Magic 1* to the next lesson.

Lesson 2 pages 6-7

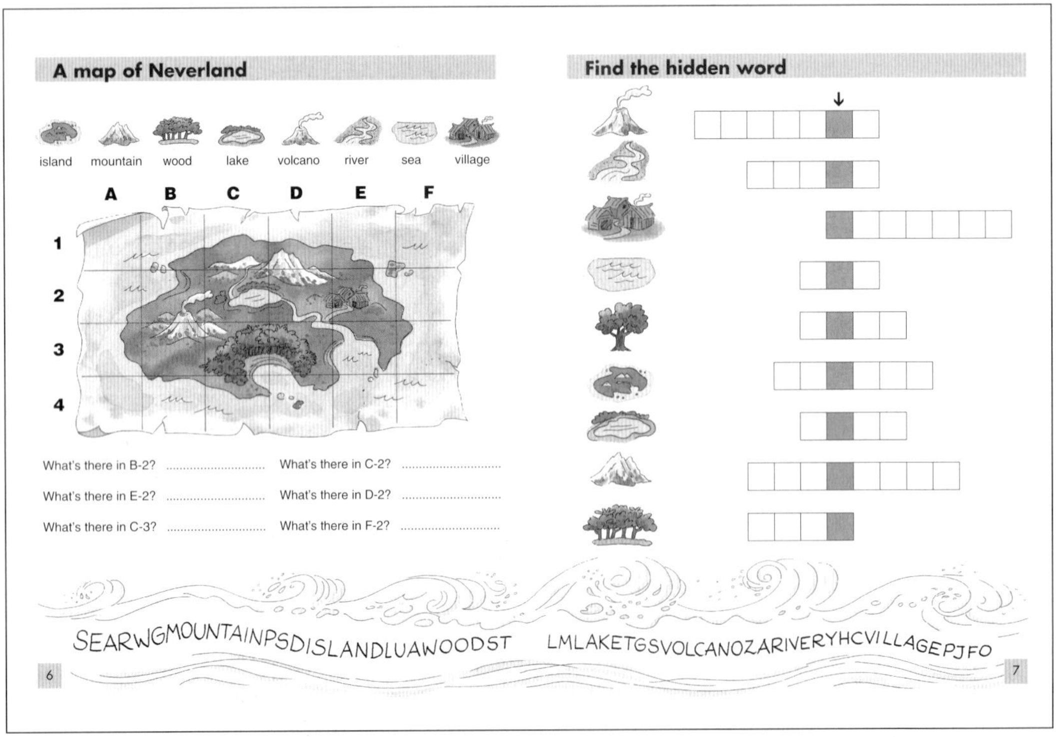

Materials: sheets of B4 paper
Vocabulary: *map, island, mountain, wood lake, volcano, river, sea, village*

I. PRESENTATION

1. A Map of Neverland (p. 6)
Tell the pupils to look at the map of Neverland on page 6. Then play the cassette with a description of the island:

Tapescript:

This is an old map of Neverland.
Neverland is a small island in Neversea.
On the island you can see a volcano, a high

mountain, a large wood, a village, a lake and a river. Would you like to visit it?

II. PRACTICE

1. Listen and point (p. 6)
Play the tape again and tell the pupils that while they are listening they must touch the parts of the island as they are mentioned on the cassette. The illustrated vocabulary will also help them.

2. What is it?
Point to the pictures of the various parts of the island saying: *What is it?*
The pupils answer individually: *It's a/an .....*
In this way you can correct any pronunciation difficulties.

3. Answer the questions (p. 6)
Read out the questions underneath the map, to provide the correct pronunciation of the letters of the alphabet. The pupils answer all together.

4. See the words in your mind
Ask the students to look carefully at the pictures with the words underneath (top page 6) for five minutes.
The children have to try to remember the spelling of each word by closing their eyes and trying to see it mentally. When the time is up, tell the children to cover the words.

5. Find the hidden word (p. 7)
Tell the pupils that they have three minutes to write the right word in the grid on page 7 relating to each picture. If the words are written correctly, the word *Neverland* will appear vertically.
The pupils correct their own mistakes with a pen of a different colour. The first person to give the solution and to have written all the words correctly is the winner.

III. REVISION

1. Word flowers
Tell the pupils to get into pairs and hand out the sheets of white B4 paper. The students must then copy this image in the middle of the sheet of paper:

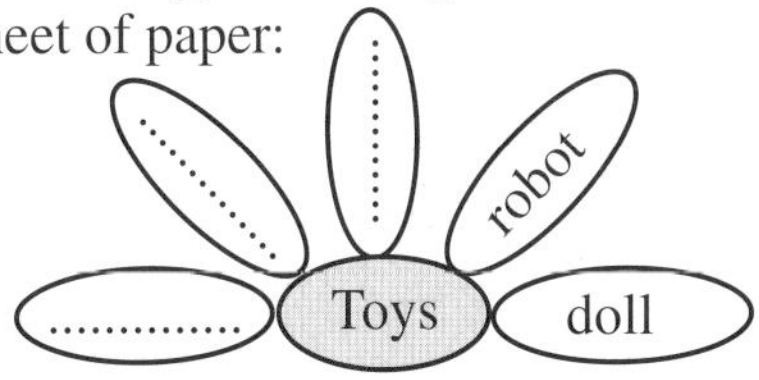

Write different categories on the blackboard (*colours, numbers 1 to 10, numbers in tens, objects in the classroom, wild animals, family members, etc.*) and assign one to each pair. The pupils write the category in the centre of the flower.
With the help of *Magic 1*, the pupils have to look for words to put in the "petals". Besides revising spelling, this activity produces material, which can be hung on the walls and be used as a reference for the students.

IV. HOMEWORK

1. Answer the questions (p. 6)
The pupils have to answer the questions as they did during the lesson.

2. Find the words in the sea (p. 6-7)
The students have to circle the words they recognize in the strip of letters.

3. Draw your own island
On a sheet of paper, the pupils draw an imaginary island with as many lakes, rivers, villages etc. as they wish.

Unit 1 - Back to Neverland

Lesson 1 pages 8-9

Materials: one poster-size sheet of paper
Functions: introducing somebody else; introducing yourself; describing yourself
Structures: *This is ..., These are ..., I'm ..., We're ...*
Vocabulary: *tall, short, thin, fat*
Phonology: /s/, /ʃ/, /t/, /θ/

I. WARM-UP

1. "Hello" chain
Ask the children to tap out the rhythm by first clapping their hands above their heads and then on their knees as they say all together:
One, two! One, two!
To the same rhythm greet the children and get them to return the greeting:
Hello, children!
Hello, teacher!
Afterwards, explain that as the class continues to tap out the rhythm each child, in turn, has to say hello to the person on his/her right saying:
Hello, (name of classmate)!

II. HOMEWORK

1. Answer the questions (p. 6)
Ask one pupil to read out the question and another to read out the answer.
In B-2 there's a volcano.
In E-2 there's a village.
In C-3 there's a wood.

In C-2 there's a lake.
In D-2 there's a river.
In F-2 there's an island.

2. Find the words in the sea (p. 6-7)
Ask one pupil to read out the words that he/she has found.
(Sea, mountain, island, wood, lake, volcano, river, village).

3. Draw your own island
Ask one pupil to show his/her picture to the class. Then ask:
How many volcanoes are there?
How many woods/lakes/rivers/villages/ mountains are there?
The child then answers:
There is/there are....
Repeat the activity with other members of the class to stress the pronunciation of the plural forms of the new vocabulary.

III. REMEMBER

Take the opportunity to quickly revise the plural forms introduced during the previous academic year.
Write the following words on the blackboard and ask the students if they can remember the spelling of the plural form: *school, potato, butterfly.*

IV. A POSTER: Plural words

You could suggest the class make a poster containing the plural form of the words they come across. The pupils illustrate the meaning with a drawing or newspaper cutting.
The suffix of the plural word should be written or circled in red.
The class will be able to reflect on the different plural forms they come across during the course of the year.

V. PRESENTATION: Back to Neverland

1. Look and answer
Tell the students to open their books at pages 8 and 9 and to look at the pictures carefully.
Then ask the following questions in L1:
- Where are Peter, Helen, David and Floppy?
- What do you think is written on the banner?
- Are Peter's friends happy to see him?
- What do they do afterwards?

Then ask some questions in English to revise the structures that the class already know. Tell the class to answer all together or individually:
- *Where are Peter, Helen, David and Floppy?*
- *How many children welcome Peter?*
- *How many girls are there?*
- *How many boys are there?*
- *Is Peter happy?*

2. Close your eyes and listen
Tell the class to close their eyes while they listen to the tape and to concentrate on the words they hear.
Afterwards, the pupils say which structures they recognized.

3. Mime the words
This time, as they hear the dialogue, the children pretend that they are speaking by moving their lips. They can follow the dialogue in their books.

4. Listen and repeat
Check that everybody has understood the dialogue, especially the new adjectives (*tall, short, thin, fat*).
Play the cassette again telling the children to repeat after each phrase.

VI. PRACTICE

1. Describe yourself
Using the adjectives *tall, short, thin* and *fat*

tell the students to take it in turns to describe themselves using the structure:
I'm (name), *I'm* (suitable adjective).
Introduce the term *slim*, which means well-proportioned and is not quite as strong as *thin*, which means that somebody is all skin and bones.

2. A traditional rhyme: "Go to bed late"
Introduce this rhyme, which is also a proverb:
Go to bed late,
stay very small.
Go to bed early,
grow very tall.
Explain the meaning of the rhyme and stress the difference between *small* and *short*. In this way, you will enrich the pupils' vocabulary relating to physical appearance.
Point out *late* and the opposite *early*.
Tell the students to copy the rhyme into their exercise books and to illustrate it for homework.

3. Who's who
Ask the pupils the following questions about the people in the dialogue. First ask the questions slowly, then more quickly.
The children answer referring to the text.

- *Who's tall and thin?*	*Teddy.*
- *Who's short and thin?*	*Tommy.*
- *Who's fat?*	*Pit/Pat.*
- *Who's very tall?*	*Toby.*
- *Who's short?*	*Sammy.*

4. Words and sounds
Write the following words on the blackboard:
short/small
thin/tall
to highlight the different phonetic sounds:
sh /ʃ/ and s /s/
th /θ/ and t /t/.

VII. HOMEWORK

1. Read the dialogue (p. 8-9)
The pupils must read the dialogue carefully so that they will be prepared to act out the story during the following lesson.

2. Learn the rhyme by heart
Tell the pupils to learn the rhyme *"Go to bed late"* by heart adding explanatory movements as they wish.

Lesson 2 pages 10-11

Functions: describing oneself in the first person singular and plural
Structures: *I've got..., We've got ...*
Vocabulary: *eyes, hair*

I. WARM-UP

1. Right or wrong?
Get the pupils to listen to a brief summary of this unit containing some mistakes. As the pupils recognize a mistake they must clap their hands.
Then correct the mistakes. If if you wish, get the pupils to correct the sentence.
For example:
The twins are in Neverland. Neverland is a mountain (clap) oh, sorry, it's an island. Floppy is not in Neverland (clap) oh, sorry, he is in Neverland ....

II. CHECKING HOMEWORK

1. Act the dialogue
Ask three volunteers to act out the dialogue in front of the class with their textbooks. They should pay partucular attention to the pronunciation and intonation, as they make the dialogue realistic with appropriate gestures.

2. Tell the rhyme
Get the pupils to recite the rhyme *"Go to bed late"* all together. Then ask a volunteer to recite it individually in front of the class.

III. PRESENTATION
Physical description

1. A game: Brown hair, stand up!
Introduce the words *hair* and *eyes* by

touching your hair and eyes and repeating the words a number of times.
Revise a few actions such as *turn around, stand up, clap your hands, snap your fingers, stretch your arms, touch your nose.*
Explain that you will ask the children with a particular hair colour or colour of eyes to perform a given action, for example:
Brown eyes, stand up!
Blue eyes, clap your hands!
Blond hair stand up and turn around!
You could also introduce the expressions: *dark hair, fair hair.*

2. Describe your hair and eyes: I've got ...
Introduce the structure to be practised by describing yourself:
I've got (colour) hair and (colour) eyes.
Write the structure on the blackboard and ask each pupil to describe himself/herself according to the example.

IV. PRACTICE

1. A message from space
To practise the structure relating to physical descriptions in the first person singular, you could get the children to play this game. By changing your voice and making what you say in L2 as clear as possible, pretend that you are a Martian from a faraway planet and describe yourself. During the description, the pupils draw a picture of you in their exercise books. Afterwards, the children show their pictures and decide which one is closest to your description.
If you want you can ask one member of the class to pretend to be a Martian and to provide a strange description of himself/herself.

2. Who am I? Who are we?
Listen and point (p. 10-11)
Play the tape and get the pupils to point at the person who is being described.

Tapescript:

I'm tall and thin. I've got blue eyes and red hair. Who am I? - ***You're Teddy.***
I'm short and thin. I've got brown eyes and blond hair. Who am I? - ***You're Tommy.***
We're fat. We've got blue eyes and brown hair. Who are we? - ***You're Pit and Pat.***
I'm very tall. I've got black eyes and black hair. Who am I? - ***You're Toby.***
I'm short. I've got blue eyes and black hair. Who am I? - ***You're Sammy.***

3. Describe the twins: They've got ...
To practise the structure *they've got,* describe David and Helen, starting like this:
David and Helen are twins.
They're .... They've got ...
Get the pupils to finish the sentences. Write the complete sentences on the blackboard and tell the children to copy them into their exercise books.

4. Who are they?
Introduce the following game. Get the children to stand in a circle, then say:
They're (tall). They've got (colour) hair.
Those children to whom the description applies take one step forwards into the middle of the circle.
One pupil then continues the game.

V. HOMEWORK

1. Who am I? Who are we? (p. 10-11)
The pupils have to write down the description of each character in the relative speech bubble.

2. Break the code (p. 10-11)
The children must decode the message on pages 10 and 11.

3. Describe Pit and Pat
On the basis of the description of David and

Helen that the pupils have already copied in their exercise books, tell the students to describe Pit and Pat.

4. Describe yourself
On a small piece of paper the pupils write a description of themselves in capital letters.

For example:
I'm tall and thin. I've got blue eyes and black hair. Who am I?
The descriptions will be used for a game during the following lesson.

Lesson 3 pages 12-13

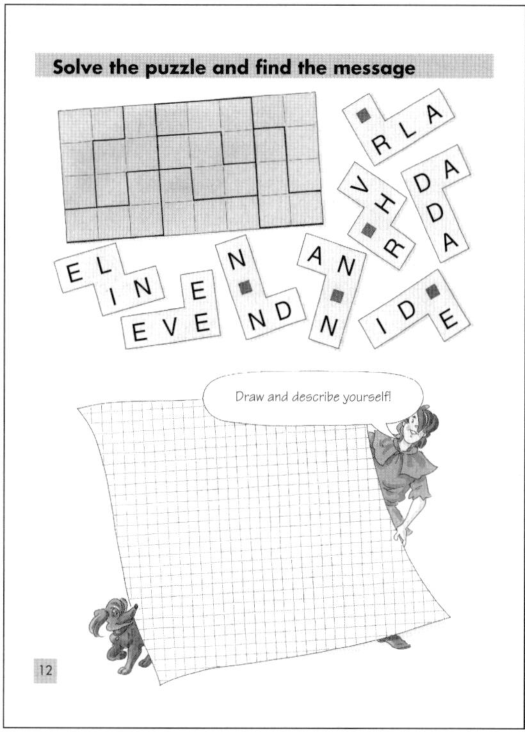

Materials: a drawing of a body on a poster-size sheet of strong white paper; names of different parts of the body on sticky labels; one thick felt-tip pen
Functions: recognizing parts of the body
Vocabulary: *fingers, toes, ears, nose, arms, legs, hands, feet, mouth*

I. CHECKING HOMEWORK

1. Who am I? Who are we? (p. 10-11)
The pupils exchange books and check that their partners have filled in the speech bubbles correctly.
In the meantime, walk around the classroom to check that there are no problems.

2. Break the code (p. 10-11)
Ask a pupil to read out the message (*Peter is back*).

3. Describe Pit and Pat
Ask a few students to read out their descriptions of Pit and Pat as you walk around the classroom checking on the others' homework.

II. CONSOLIDATION

1. The description game
Collect the small pieces of paper prepared at home after getting the pupils to write their names in pencil on the back. Shuffle the pieces of paper and place them on your desk with the description facing upwards.
Call out one child who, having chosen a piece of paper and read the contents, must guess who wrote the description.
If he/she guesses correctly, then the other classmate comes up to your desk to continue the game. If, however, the pupil's guess is wrong, he/she has to do a small forfeit suggested by the person who was mistakenly named.
The forfeit could be to perform an action (*touch a book*), to repeat an action a number of times (*turn around five times*) or to answer a question (*When's your birthday?*).
Then choose another pupil to continue the activity. At the end of the game give the pieces of paper back to the respective pupils.

III. LET'S SING A SONG

1. "I've got ten fingers" (p. 13)
Provide a description of your body in the form of a song.

2. Close your eyes and listen
Tell the children to close their eyes and to concentrate on the words of the song.
Once they have listened to the tape the pupils say which words they have understood.

3. Listen and show
Let the children listen to the song again as you point to the various parts of the body.
The next time they hear the tape, ask them to do the same.

4. Look and listen
Get the children to open their books at page 13 and as they listen to the tape they can read the written text.

5. Mime the words
The children pretend to sing the song moving only their lips without producing any sounds.

6. Let's sing together
The pupils sing the song all together accompanied by suitable gestures.

IV. PRACTICE

1. A poster: the body
Pin up the picture of the body so that everybody can see it. Touch the body and say:
This is the body.
Then write the sentence on the sheet of paper with a thick felt-tip pen.
After handing out the sticky labels with the vocabulary relating to the body ask:
Who's got the (hand)?
The pupil holding the sticky label with that word answers: *Me!* and sticks it on the poster in the right place.
If you consider it the case, you could extend the vocabulary relating to the human body by introducing other words which are presented in *Unit 3*.

V. REMEMBER

Tell the children to open their books at page 13 and to underline the plural forms of the parts of the body in red, and the singular forms in blue.
Point out that some words have irregular plural forms as in the case of *feet*.
Tell the pupils to write the singular form *foot* next to it.
Ask the children to read out the words they have underlined. Afterwards get them to open their exercise books and to divide one page into two columns. In the first column they will write the singular form of the words and in the other the plural form:

Singular	*Plural*
....	*fingers*
....	*toes*
....	*ears*
....	*eyes*
nose	....
....	*arms*
mouth	....

At the end of the activity check all the words.

VI. HOMEWORK

1. Solve the puzzle and find the message (p. 12)
The children have to solve the puzzle and find the message.

2. Draw and describe yourself (p. 12)
The children have to draw a picture of themselves in the space on page 12. Then they must copy the description of themselves beneath the picture used in the *Description game.*

3. Learn the song by heart
The pupils have to learn the song on page 13 by heart.

Unit 2 - Peter's family

Lesson 1 pages 14-15

Functions: asking and giving information about somebody's health; asking and saying where somebody comes from (first person singular and plural)
Structures: *How are you? Fine, thanks (thank you), Where are you from? I'm from ... We're from ... What about you? I'm from ..., too*
Vocabulary: *from, Great Britain, Greece, Germany, live, without, too.*

I. WARM-UP

1. Sing the song
Get the children to sing together *"I've got ten fingers"* accompanying it with suitable gestures. Then ask a few volunteers to sing and mime the song in front of the class.

II. CHECKING HOMEWORK

1. Solve the puzzle and find the message (p. 12)
Ask one pupil to read out the message in the puzzle. The message is:
David and Helen are in Neverland.

2. Draw and describe yourself (p. 12)
Walk around the classroom checking that everybody has done this activity correctly.

III. PRESENTATION: Peter's family

1. Look and answer
Tell the children to open their books at pages 14 and 15 and to look at the pictures carefully.

Then ask in L1:
- What do you think Peter Pan is doing in the first picture?
- What do you think is wrong with Floppy in the last picture?

After having heard what the class has to say, get the children to number the pictures from 1 to 10.
Then ask some simple questions in L2 using structures that the pupils already know:
- *How many girls are there in picture number 1?*
  And how many boys?
- *Who's there in picture number 2?*
- *Is Teddy in picture number 6?*
- *How many legs can you see near Floppy in picture number 10?*

If necessary help the pupils with the answers.

2. Close your eyes and listen
Tell the students to close their eyes as they listen to the cassette and to concentrate on the words and structures they hear.
Afterwards, they must say which ones they already know.

3. Mime the words
Following the text in their books, the pupils pretend to be the characters in the book and repeat the dialogue by moving only their lips.

4. Listen and repeat
After checking that everybody has understood the dialogue, get the pupils to listen to the tape again and repeat after each phrase.

IV. PRACTICE:

1. Chain game
Get the children to repeat the following short dialogue a few times:
How are you? Fine, thanks (thank you).
Tell the pupils that they are going to play a chain game in which one child asks the person on his/her right the question and the classmate replies. The latter then turns to the person on his/her right and they repeat the dialogue.

2. Let's act
Ask two volunteers to come up to the front of the class to act out the dialogue.
The pupils choose a name for themselves (either the English equivalent of their name or a new name) and then pretend to meet one another by chance saying:

Jack: *Hello, Susan.*
Susan: *Hello, Jack. How are you?*
Jack: *Fine, thanks.*

After getting other pairs to practise the short informal dialogue tell one girl to take the part of the teacher, Miss Black. Get another pupil to meet Miss Black and to greet her formally:

John: *Good morning, Miss Black.*
Miss Black: *Good morning , John.*
How are you?
John: *Fine, thank you.*

Call up other pairs of students, changing the teacher's name (Mr White, Mrs Pink).

V. CONSOLIDATION

1. Think about a Martian
This activity is similar to the one introduced in the previous unit (re. U1.L2.IV,1) but here it is based on written production.
Tell the pupils to look at the pictures of the Martian they drew during the previous lesson.
Ask them whether their pictures correspond to what they think a creature from outer space might look like.
Encourage the children to be as imaginative as possible letting them express themselves in L1.

2. Draw a Martian
Tell the children to imagine what a Martian might look like and to draw one.

3. Make your Martian describe itself
Ask the children to draw a speech bubble next to the Martian in which the strange creature introduces and describes itself.
You could draw and colour in one of these imaginary creatures on one side of the blackboard and fill in a speech bubble as a model for the pupils:

Hello! My name's ... and I'm from Mars. I'm tall and fat.
I've got one purple head, three yellow eyes, one red nose, one pink mouth and five green teeth; I've got four orange arms, four white hands, eight fingers, six brown legs and six black feet.

Underline the structures that the students should include in their descriptions while the vocabulary relating to numbers, colours and parts of the body will vary according to the individual pictures.
Once all the children have finished their description, ask them to take it in turns to read out what they have written to the rest of the class.

VI. HOMEWORK

1. Read the dialogue (p. 14-15)
The pupils must read the dialogue in *Unit 2* carefully so that they will be ready to act it out during the next lesson.

2. Draw the flag you like
Tell the pupils to choose one of the flags on page 16 and to draw it on a sheet of paper.

3. Collect some pictures
Ask the children to cut out two or three pictures of famous people from magazines or newspapers.
The pictures should be accompanied by some basic information such as age, nationality and profession.
In their exercise books the pupils must write a brief presentation in the first person singular using the following suggestions that they have copied from the blackboard:
My name's ....
I'm from ....
I'm (age).
I'm (tall/short/thin/slim/fat).
I've got (blue) eyes and (blond) hair.
In this way the pupils can practise the new structures and put together material for a poster entitled: *FAMOUS PEOPLE.*

Lesson 2 pages 16-17

Materials: the flags prepared by the pupils at home
Functions: asking about and saying one's nationality
Structures: *I'm French, He's Greek*
Vocabulary: *France, Norway, Spain, Bonn, Paris, Madrid, Athens, Oslo, Spanish, French, Greek, British, Norwegian*

I. CHECKING HOMEWORK

1. Act the dialogue (p. 14-15)
Ask a few volunteers to act out the dialogue with their textbooks open and telling them to pay partucular attention to pronunciation, intonation and gestures.

2. Collect the pictures
Collect the pictures of famous people that the pupils have brought to class, saying that you have to check through them before using the pictures.
Choose no more that five or six representative personalities (a singer, an actor, a tennis player, a TV presenter etc.).

II. PRESENTATION: Countries

1. Where are they from? (p. 16)
Tell the children to open their books at page 16 and to look at each country's flag.
Get the pupils to repeat the names of the countries a few times to make sure their pronunciation is correct.

III. PRACTICE

1. Playing with flags (1)

Ask the pupils to show you their sheets of paper with the picture of a flag. When you ask a pupil: *Where are you from?* he/she answers saying *I'm from...* (followed by the name of the country represented by the flag).
To practise the use of the third person singular, tell the pupils to hold up their flags. Ask a volunteer to come up to the front of the class and, pointing at another member of the class, ask the child by your desk:
Where is he/she from?
The child then answers: *He/she's from ...* (followed by the name of the country represented by the flag).
As a final exercise, to practise the plural forms, get the students to form groups (one for each nation). Ask a pupil from a different group to answer the question:
Where are they from?

IV. PRESENTATION: Capital cities

1. What's the capital of ...?

Write the name of a country on the blackboard and ask:
What's the capital of (nation)?
Check that everybody has understood the meaning of the word capital and get the pupils to answer in L1.
Supply the English equivalent of the names of the capitals and write them on the blackboard next to the respective country.
Tell the children to look at the names of the cities carefully as they will be asked to write them during the next activity.

V. PRACTICE

1. Listen and complete (p. 16)

Ask the pupils to listen to the tape on which Helen talks about her new friends saying the capital city they come from and their nationality.
The children must concentrate on the new words they hear, particularly on the names of the capitals. Before you play the cassette a second time, rub out the words on the blackboard and tell the children to open their books at page 16 and to complete the sentences by writing in the names of the capitals as they hear them on the tape. Play the cassette a third time during which the children check what they have written.

Tapescript:

Teddy's from Bonn. He's German.
Tommy's from Paris. He's French.
Toby's from Madrid. He's Spanish.
Sammy's from Athens. He's Greek.
David and Helen are from London.
They're British.
Pit and Pat are from Oslo. They're Norwegian.

Afterwards, you could ask some questions to check comprehension, such as:
Where's Teddy from?
Where are David and Helen from?
Is Toby from Madrid?
Are Pit and Pat from Athens?
In this way, you can check the pupils' ability to reply using both long and short answers.

VI. HOMEWORK

1. Where are they from? (p. 16)

The pupils complete the sentences in the speech bubbles.

2. What's the answer? (p. 17)

In class, ask the children to take it in turns to read out the phrases in the speech bubbles on page 17 to check that their pronunciation and intonation are correct.
Get the pupils match to the questions and answers for homework.

Lesson 3 pages 18-19

The hidden countries and nationalities

F	R	A	N	C	E	P	T	O	G	F	L
M	G	F	N	O	R	W	E	G	I	A	N
G	R	R	O	G	E	R	M	A	N	Y	B
X	E	E	T	G	R	E	E	K	O	A	R
P	E	N	D	A	B	C	X	W	Y	L	I
T	C	C	F	S	P	A	I	N	M	T	T
H	E	H	G	E	R	M	A	N	X	T	I
L	M	G	N	O	R	W	A	Y	P	Q	S
S	P	A	N	I	S	H	R	S	O	G	H
G	R	E	A	T	B	R	I	T	A	I	N

Find the rhymes

you	now
Pat	pen
where	too
how	fat
ten	there

18

Let's sing!

Where are you from?
I'm from France.
What about you?
I'm French, too.

Where are you from?
I'm from Germany.
What about you?
I'm German, too.

Where are you from?
I'm from Italy.
What about you?
I'm Italian, too.

Where are you from?
I'm from Great Britain.
What about you?
I'm British, too.

19

Materials: one poster-size sheet of paper; pictures of famous people (brought in by the children); felt-tip pens
Revision of **functions** and **structures** relating to physical description and where someone comes from
Phonology: /u:/, /ae/, /eə/, /au/, /e/.

I. CHECKING HOMEWORK

1. Where are they from? (p. 16)
On the blackboard, write *I'm from ...* and ask the children to check the spelling. Correct the sentences orally.

2. What's the answer (p. 17)
Tell the pupils to check their answers as they listen to the cassette.

Tapescript

What's your name?	*My name's Andy.*
How old are you?	*I'm ten.*
Where are you from?	*I'm from Norway.*
Are you from Spain?	*No, I'm not.*
Are you hungry?	*Yes, I am.*
What time is it?	*It's six o'clock.*
What's that?	*It's a squirrel.*

II. REVISION

1. Playing with flags (2)
In order to revise some of the structures presented in the activity on page 17, get the

children to use the flags they have prepared for the next game.
Divide the class into two teams. The members of each team have to fold up the piece of paper with the picture of the flag so that it can not be seen. Collect the pieces of paper, shuffle them and redistribute them. Each child looks to see what nationality he/she must assume without letting the others see his/her flag.
Each member of the team has only one guess to find out the nationality of a classmate in the other team. The following exchange of words should be used:
Where are you from? Are you from (Spain)?
Yes, I am/No, I'm not.
If the answer is affermative, then the classmate will be "captured".
If the answer is negative, the situation remains unchanged.
You could set a time limit and the winning team is the one to have "captured" the most members of the opposite team.

III. THINK: adjectives of nationalities

1. Teddy's from Bonn. He's German (p.16)
Tell the children to open their books at page 16 and to notice how the structure *I'm from ...* can be followed either by the name of the country or by the city someone comes from.
After reading the exercise (previously completed with the names of capitals), ask the pupils what other form can be used to express where someone comes from. They should not find it difficult to indicate the adjectives of nationality.

IV. REMEMBER

Tell the children to draw two columns, one entitled *Countries* and the other *Nationalities* under the heading *Remember* in their exercise books. Then they copy the adjective of nationality for each country from their textbooks.

V. PRACTICE

1. Match it quickly
Call out a country and the students, with their books open, have to reply all together with the corresponding adjective. Gradually, increase the speed of the game.
Afterwards, name the adjectives with the pupils calling out the countries.
Finally, alternate the adjectives and the countries.
When you consider it the right stage, tell the children to close their exercise books.

VI. CONSOLIDATION

1. A poster: Famous People
Pin up the poster-size sheet of paper at a suitable height for the children and ask one pupil to write the title: *Famous People.*
In the meantime, show the class the types of personality you have chosen for the poster and ask the pupils with descriptions relating to a particular profession to form a group.
Show everybody the first picture and ask the child who brought it in to stick it on the poster.
If there is more than one description, read them all out and then select one.
One member of the group will be in charge of copying the description into a speech bubble drawn on a sheet of paper.
They should then cut it out and stick onto the poster next to the personality it refers to.
Advise the children to leave a space of at least three lines inside the speech bubble so that more information can be added (description of clothes, skills etc.).

Leave plenty of space beneath each personality for questions and answers in the third person singular.

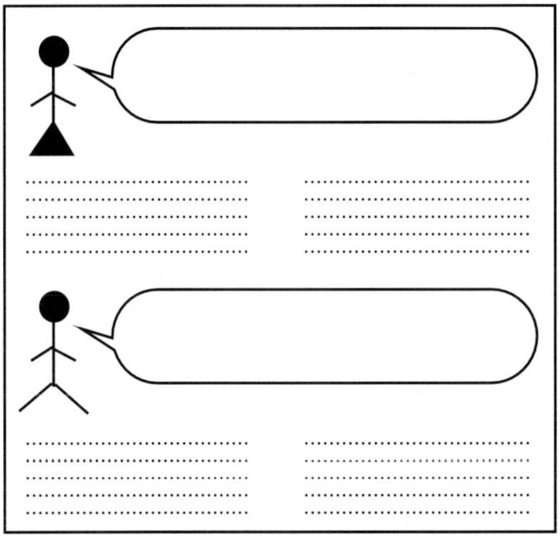

2. Find the rhymes (p. 18)

Tell the children to open their books at page 18, to read the words silently and to join the ones that rhyme with a line.

Afterwards, ask the pupils to listen to the tape and to check their answers.

Tapescript:

You	*too*
Pat	*fat*
Where	*there*
How	*now*
Ten	*pen*

Get the children to repeat the rhyming words all together.

VII. LET'S SING A SONG

1. "Where are you from?" (p. 19)

Before playing the tape, ask the children to imagine the setting of the song (a party where children of different nationalities meet).

2. Close your eyes and listen

Tell the children to close their eyes and to concentrate on the words as they listen to the song.

After playing the tape a second time, the pupils say which countries the children in the song come from.

They will probably not have any difficulty in recognizing the two new words: *Italy* and *Italian*.

3. Listen and point

The children have to point to the respective flag as each child sings.

4. Look and listen

This time the pupils follow the text in their books as they listen to the cassette.

5. Mime the words

The students pretend to sing the song by moving their lips without producing any sounds.

6. Let's sing

Get the children to sing the song together.

VIII. HOMEWORK

1. The hidden countries (p. 18)

The children have to find all the words relating to European countries and nationalities.

2. Learn the song by heart (p. 19)

The children have to learn the song by heart.

Unit 3 - Hook is back

Lesson 1 pages 20-21

Materials: a map of the United Kingdom
Functions: physical descriptions in the third person singular
Structures: *He/She's ...., He/She's got ...*
Vocabulary: *terrible, pirate, long, round*

I. WARM-UP

1. Sing the song

Get the children to sing "*Where are you from?*" all together. Then ask some pairs of volunteers to each sing one verse in the form of a dialogue.

2. Write your own song

Ask the pupils to write new verses to the song in pairs by adding a new country and the respective nationality adjective.
Let them use their textbooks if necessary.

II. CHECKING HOMEWORK

1. The hidden countries (p. 18)

Ask a number of students to read out the countries and nationalities they found in the wordsearch.

III. REVISION

1. Let's speak about Britain and the British flag

Tell the children to open their books at

pages 16 and 17. On the blackboard write: *This is the ... flag* and get the pupils to complete the sentence orally by inserting the appropriate adjective according to the flag indicated.
Then ask: *What colour is it?* to which the students answer with: *It's ...*
Show the class the British flag and take the chance to talk about the United Kingdom.
On the blackboard, write: *The United Kingdom of Great Britain and Northern Ireland.*
Then translate the heading along with the students. Tell the children to look at the map and point out that the term United Kingdom includes the political union of Great Britain and Northern Ireland, and that Great Britain is divided into three countries: *Scotland, England and Wales.*
In addition, highlight the fact that each part of the United Kingdom has its own capital. Point to the cities on the map and continue your description in L2:
Look, this is Belfast. It's the capital of Northern Ireland.
And this is Edinburgh, the capital of Scotland.
The capital of Wales is Cardiff. Look, it's here.
And... What is the capital of England?
Referring to the flag, say that it is called the *Union Jack* and that it is the product of the union of the flags of England, Scotland and Northern Ireland. The Welsh flag does not appear in the *Union Jack*, because when the Union flag was created (1801), Wales was no longer an independent monarchy having been annexed some time before to the English monarchy.
You could draw the flags on the blackboard and supply a brief comment:
the white flag with a red cross: *the cross of St. George, England;*
the white flag with a diagonal red cross: *the cross of St. Patrick, Ireland;*
the blue flag with a diagonal white cross: *the cross of St. Andrew, Scotland.*
Then draw the Union Jack and tell the children to copy what you have put on the blackboard into their exercise books.
If you want to mention the characteristics of the Welsh flag, say that it is divided horizontally into two parts: the upper part is white, and the lower part is green and in the centre there is a white dragon.
The flag is the emblem of *St. David.*

IV. PRESENTATION: Hook is back!

1. Look and answer

Tell the pupils to open their books at pages 20 and 21 and to look at the pictures carefully. Then ask in L1:

- What are the children in Neverland worried about?
- Who are in the pictures that Tommy shows?
- Why is David afraid?
- Why is Peter laughing in the last picture?

Get the children to number the pictures from one to nine and then ask some questions in English which the pupils answer all together:

- *How many children can you see in picture number 1?*
- *Who can you see behind Peter's leg in picture number 3?*
- *Are there nine children in picture number 4?*
- *How many hands can you count in picture number 5?*
- *What has Peter got in his hands in picture number 9?*

2. Close your eyes and listen

Tell the children to close their eyes and to concentrate on what they hear on the cassette.
Afterwards, ask them which words or phrases they recognized.

3. Mime the words

The students follow the dialogue with their textbooks open and pretend to be the characters in the story by moving their lips without producing any sounds.

4. Listen and repeat
Check that everybody has understood the dialogue. Play the tape again and tell the children to repeat each phrase after it is said.

V. THINK

1. Adjective position
Get the pupils to look at the descriptions of Hook and Smythe carefully and to underline the sentences in which two adjectives appear before the noun.
For example, in the description of Hook it says: *He's got long black hair.*
Ask the children if they can identify the order of the adjectives: first the adjective of size (*long, short*) and then the colour (*black, white*) or first the shape (*round*) and then the colour (*red*).

VI. PRACTICE

1. Let's play with adjectives
Draw the following chart on the blackboard and ask the pupils to suggest words they know to be placed in the appropriate column. Give each column a different colour.

size	*shape*	*colour*	*body parts*
long	*round*	*brown*	*hair*
short	....	*white*	*eyes*
small		*black*	*moustache*
big		*red*	*nose*
little		*blond*	*mouth*
....		....	....

Then each pupil takes a small piece of paper and writes the word you suggest in the corresponding colour. Make sure that the number of words in the table is the same as the number of students in class.
Write a sentence in L1 on the blackboard describing one of the characters in the story, for example:
Hook has got a long black moustache.
Tell the children with the words needed to form the sentence (*long/moustache/black*) on their piece of paper to come to the front of the class and to stand in the appropriate order.
Read out the sentence in English.
Start saying: *Hook's got a ...* and each pupil completes the sentence by reading out his/her word. When the students have understood the mechanism, let them suggest the sentences.

2. Describe your deskmate
Each pupil has to describe his/her deskmate according to the model provided in the dialogue relating to the descriptions of Hook and Smythe. Point out that if the deskmate is a girl then *she* must be used instead of *he*.

VII. HOMEWORK

1. Read the dialogue (p. 20-21)
The pupils read the dialogue carefully so that they will be prepared to act it out in class during the next lesson.

Lesson 2 pages 22-23

Materials: white sheets of paper
Functions: describing feelings
Structures: *He/She's ..., He/She isn't ...*
Vocabulary: *happy, sad, surprised, tired, angry, scared*

I. CHECKING HOMEWORK

1. Act the dialogue (p. 22-23)
Ask a few volunteers to act out the dialogue in front of the class with their books open for reference. Make sure that their pronunciation and intonation is correct and that they use suitable gestures.

II. CONSOLIDATION

1. Famous people: questions and answers
Show the class the picture of a famous person from the poster (ref: U2.L3.VI,1) and ask some questions such as:
Who is he/she?
Where is he/she from?
How old is he/she?
Is he/she tall or short?
Has he/she got (colour) hair/eyes?
The pupils could answer either individually or all together.
Then tell the children to work in pairs and give each pair a different famous person. After writing on the blackboard the above questions, with a line in the place of the personal pronoun, ask one pupil from each pair to copy the questions on to a sheet of paper inserting the appropriate pronoun.

The other pupil in each pair has to supply the answers, using the information in the speech bubble relating to the particular person.
Both sheets of paper will then be glued onto the poster beneath the famous person they describe.
Hand out the remaining pictures to the pupils (one each). They glue the pictures into their exercise books and write questions and answers as in the example on the poster.

III. PRESENTATION: Feelings

1. Mime a feeling on your face
Introduce a miming game in which you change your facial expression by passing your hand over your face.
At the same time say:
I'm happy/sad/...
The pupils imitate the facial expression and repeat the corresponding phrase.
After a few goes, tell the children to take it in turns to carry out the game in front of the class.

IV. PRACTICE

1. Look and complete (p. 23)
Tell the students to open their books at pages 22 and 23 and to look carefully at the expressions of the children in the coloured sweaters.
Ask one child to read out the first example of the exercise on page 23 and explain that he/she has to complete the sentence according to the feeling expressed by the character in the picture.
Allow enough time for all the children to finish the exercise.
When they have all finished ask a few pupils to read out their sentences.

2. I'm happy when ....
After making sure that all the students understand the meaning of the words that express feelings and states of mind write on the blackboard:
I'm .... when I ....
and at the same time say:
I'm scared when I see a snake!
Ask each pupil to say a phrase using the proposed structure, completing it as they wish.

3. A guessing game
Call two children up to the blackboard and get them to stand one behind the other. The child in front has to mime an expression to the class and the pupil behind has two chances to guess the expression by asking:
Is he/she happy?
The rest of the class answer either individually or all together using short answers.
After the second guess, it is the other person's turn.

VI. HOMEWORK

1. Read and complete (p. 22)
The children have to match the right description to the characters by writing in the appropriate spaces.

2. Find some cuttings
Each pupil has to cut out pictures of people in magazines who clearly express a feeling.
The children glue the pictures into their exercise books and try to describe them physically adding the adjective relating to their facial expression:
He/She's got ... eyes and ... hair.
He/She's (tall/thin/...).
He/She's (scared/sad/...).
Remind the pupils to pay attentio to their use of *he/she*.

Lesson 3 pages 24-25

Materials: the poster of the human body started in Unit 1
Functions: asking about physical appearance; names of parts of the body
Structures: *What are they like?*
Vocabulary: *head, shoulders, knees, toes, ears, mouth, arms, legs, feet, hands*

I. CHECKING HOMEWORK

1. Read and complete (p. 22)
Ask one of the pupils to read out his/her description starting with:
Hook's got .../Smythe's got ...
(*Hook's got long black hair, a black moustache, big ears, one hand, blue eyes, a long nose.*
Smythe's got short white hair, a short white beard, brown eyes, a round nose).

2. Find some cuttings
Ask a few children to show the class the pictures they have cut out and to read out their descriptions. Together with the other members of the class, decide whether to add more information.

III. CONSOLIDATION

1. Role-play
Introduce a guided role-play in which the pupils recall the dialogue in Unit 3.
This activity will help them to remember the

structures and expressions.
Five volunteers take the parts of Peter, Tommy, Helen, David and the children in Neverland who speak all together (so you only need one pupil for this part).
Give short indications in L1.
To make the activity all the more theatrical, get another five volunteers to stand behind the first five actors and to prompt them with the dialogue from their textbooks in the case of difficulty.

- Peter asks what is new in Neverland.

- Tommy replies that Hook is back.

- Helen asks who Hook is.

- David answers that Hook is a pirate.

- The children in Neverland stress that Hook is a terrible pirate.

- Tommy says that Hook is tall and thin. He has got long black hair and a long black moustache. He has got blue eyes, big ears, a long nose and ... only one hand.
  He adds that Smythe is his friend. He is short and fat. He has got short white hair and a short white beard. He has got brown eyes and a round red nose.

- David makes an exclamation of fear when he sees the shadow of a man with a hook and says that it is Hook. Then he turns around shouting for help. He says that the pirates are here.

- Peter tells him to calm down: it's only the shadow of a banana.

III. PRESENTATION AND PRACTICE

1. What are they like? (p. 24)
Tell the pupils to open their books at page 24.
Point out the expression: *What are they like?* used when asking about someone's physical appearance; in this case the two pirates.
Do the exercise orally in class getting all the children to participate.

2. Listen and draw (p. 24)
Ask the students to listen to the description of the pirate One Eye saying:
Now listen to the cassette.
What is the Pirate One Eye like?
The second time they hear the tape they have to draw the pirate in their exercise books according to the description given.

Tapescript:

The Pirate One Eye isn't very tall.
He's short and thin.
He's got short red hair and a red beard, too.
He's got a round nose, a large mouth and... only one blue eye.
That's why his name's Pirate One Eye.

Play the tape again so that the pupils can check or finish their drawings.
Walk around the classroom to make sure there are no problems. You could then ask some questions:
Is the Pirate One Eye tall or short?
Is he thin, slim or fat?
What colour is his hair?
What colour is his beard?
Is the pirate's nose long or round?
Is the pirate's mouth large or small?
What colour is the pirate's eye?

IV. PRESENTATION: Parts of the body

1. Let's do some gymnastics
Tell the pupils to stand up as they are going to do some gymnastics. Give the instructions in English and do the appropriate movements to illustrate the meaning:

Shake your shoulders,
Stamp your feet,
Bend your knees,
Stretch your arms.

Clap your hands,
Shake your head,
Touch your toes,
And pull your ... nose.

Touch the parts of your body as you name them changing the tone of your voice when you say the new words.
Then the children perform the movements as you repeat the phrases all together.
Write the actions on the blackboard and ask the pupils to copy the sequence into their exercise books.

2. Complete the body poster
On the basis of the new vocabulary, complete the body poster (ref. U1.L3.IV,1) by writing the new words next to the corresponding parts of the body.

V. LET'S SING A SONG

1. "Head and Shoulders" (p. 25)
Tell the children that the song they are going to hear has the new words they have just learnt.

2. Close your eyes and listen
Ask the pupils to close their eyes and to concentrate on the pronunciation of the words.

3. Listen and touch
Get the children to stand up near their desks and say:
Look at me and do what I do!
Indicate the parts of the body mentioned in the song and the children must do the same.

4. Look and listen
The pupils listen to the song as they follow the text in their books.

5. Mime the words
The students pretend to sing the song by moving only their lips without producing any sounds.

6. Let's sing
At this stage, the pupils sing the song all together accompanied by the explanatory movements.

VI. HOMEWORK

1. What are they like? (p. 24)
The children have to fill in the speech bubbles relating to Smythe, with the help of the dialogue on page 21 if necessary.

2. Learn the song by heart (p. 25)
The pupils have to learn the song *"Head and Shoulders"* by heart.

3. Update the list of body parts
Ask the children to update the list of body parts in the exercise books (ref.U1.L3.V).

Unit 4 - Peter's house

Lesson 1 pages 26-27

Functions: asking and replying about possession
Structures: *Have you got a/an ...?, What have you got?*
Vocabulary: *far, up, ladder, idea*

I. WARM-UP

1. Sing the song
Ask the children to sing the song "*Head and Shoulders*" accompanied by the movements. Get them to sing the song slowly the first time and then more quickly the second time.

II. CHECKING HOMEWORK

1. What are they like? (p. 24)
Ask two students to read out the contents of the speech bubbles. Afterwards, ask a volunteer to answer the question: *What is Hook like?* with a complete description of the pirate. Tell the pupil to repeat the name instead of using the personal pronoun. Do the same activity for Smythe.

2. Update the list of body parts
Ask a member of the class to read out his/her list of words.

III. CONSOLIDATION

1. Chant the verb to have (affermative form)
As described in the *Welcome unit* (L1.II,3),

suggest the following chant to consolidate the verb *to have*, in the affermative form:
I've got, I've got, I've got
You've got, you've got, you've got
He's got, he's got
She's got, she's got
We've got
You've got
They've got

IV. PRESENTATION: Peter's house

1. Look and answer
Tell the pupils to open their books at pages 26 and 27 and to look at the pictures carefully. Then ask in L1:
- Where are Peter and his friends going?
- Where is Peter's house?
- Is Floppy happy about climbing up to Peter's house?
- How do the children get Floppy up to the tree house?

Get the children to number the pictures from 1 to 8 and ask them the following questions in English:
- *How many children can you see in picture number 1?*
- *What is Sammy like?*
- *What is Peter like?*
- *How many feet can you see in picture number 1?*
- *Who's there in picture number 2? And in picture number 3?*
- *Is Floppy near Pat?*
- *Are Pit and Pat in the tree house in picture number 6? Who's there?*
- *Are there two girls in picture number 8?*
- *Who's near the tree in picture number 8?*

2. Close your eyes and listen
Tell the children to close their eyes and to concentrate on the words they hear as they listen to the cassette. Afterwards, the pupils say which new word or phrase struck them most.

3. Mime the words
Following the dialogue in their textbooks, the students pretend to be the characters in the story and move their lips without producing any sounds as they listen to the tape.

4. Listen and repeat
Check that everybody has understood all the dialogue. As they listen to the cassette again, the pupils repeat after each phrase.

V. PRESENTATION: Have you got...?
Yes, I have/No, I haven't

1. In my pencil case ...
Explain that the structure *I've got ...* can be used when you want to express possession. Then write on the blackboard:
In my pencil case I've got ...
Tell the pupils to copy the sentence into their exercise books and to finish it once they have checked what is in their pencil cases. Walk around the classroom asking:
What have you got in your pencil case?
One pupil replies by showing the objects and counting them as in the example:
I've got (three pens, one rubber, one ruler and one pencil).
At the end of the activity, on the blackboard write the structure:
What have you got? so that the students can copy it into their exercise books.

2. Have you got ...?
Put some of the contents of your pencil case into your handbag or in a plastic bag.
Get the pupils to take it in turns to ask you a question to find out which objects you have put in the bag using the structure:
Have you got a/an ...
Reply accordingly:
Yes, I have/No, I haven't.
Your answers will give the children the opportunity to hear the short answers using to verb *to have*.

VI. CONSOLIDATION

1. The "if" game

As a way to revise the vocabulary and structures relating to physical appearance suggest the following game which requires those people with determined physical characteristics to perform a given action. For example, you could say:

- *If you're tall, stand up, sit down.*
- *If you're short, stand up, turn around, sit down.*
- *If you've got brown hair, stand up, clap your hands, sit down.*
- *If you've got blue eyes, stand up, say your name, sit down.*
- *If you've got blue eyes and brown hair, stand up, go to the door, come back, sit down.*
- *If you've got red hair, jump three times.*

Whoever makes a mistake or does not perform an action when required to do so has to pay a small penalty.

VII. HOMEWORK

1. Read the dialogue (p. 26-27)

The pupils have to read the dialogue carefully so that they will be prepared to act it out in class during the following lesson.

Lesson 2 pages 28-29

Functions: asking about possession and answering in the affirmative or negative; describing objects in the house
Structures: *Have you got ...? Yes, I have. No, I haven't.*
Vocabulary: *washbasin, chair, mirror, sofa, table, wardrobe, fridge, bath, cupboard, television, lamp, bed*

I. CHECKING HOMEWORK

1. Act the dialogue (p. 26-27)

Ask some volunteers to act out the dialogue in front of the class with their books for reference.

Make sure that their pronunciation, intonation and gestures are correct.

II. PRESENTATION: Furniture

1. What's there? (p. 28)
Tell the pupils to open their books at page 28. Point at the rooms of the house illustrated in the middle of the page saying:
What is it?
The children should answer:
It's a kitchen/bedroom/bathroom/sitting-room.

2. Listen and point (p. 28)
After reading out the names of the objects on either side of the pictures of the rooms, call them out randomly getting the children to point to the particular object.
Gradually increase the speed with which you name the objects.

III. PRACTICE

1. Answer and ask (p. 28)
Get the children to observe in which rooms the illustrated objects are to be found. Then ask one pupil:
Where's the washbasin?
He/She answers: *In the bathroom.*
He/She then turns to his/her deskmate and asks where another object is to be found.
Proceed in this way until all the objects have been named.

2. Look, listen and answer (p. 28)
Tell the pupils to listen to the cassette with their books closed. They have to answer the speaker's questions using the answers they have already practised.
You could press the pause button to give the children time to think of the answer. When you say so, everybody replies together. By pressing the pause button a second time, you will hear the voice of the second speaker with the right answers.

Tapescript:

Where can you see a washbasin?
In the bathroom.
Where can you see a chair?
In the kitchen.
Where can you see a mirror?
In the bathroom.
Where can you see a sofa?
In the sitting-room.
Where can you see a table?
In the kitchen.
Where can you see a wardrobe?
In the bedroom.
Where can you see a fridge?
In the kitchen.
Where can you see a bath?
In the bathroom.
Where can you see a cupboard?
In the kitchen.
Where can you see a television?
In the sitting-room.
Where can you see a lamp?
In the bedroom.
Where can you see a bed?
In the bedroom.

IV. CONSOLIDATION

1. Let's play bingo
Suggest a game of *Bingo* to consolidate the new vocabulary.
Tell the children to circle with a pencil five of the twelve objects illustrated on either side of page 28. Call out the name of an object and if anyone has chosen it as one of his/her five objects then he/she circles it again. Once the fifth object has been circled a second time, the student shouts out: *Bingo!*

2. A guessing game: Have you got ...?
Get the students to call to mind the structures:

Have you got...? Yes, I have/No, I haven't.
Ask two pupils to come up to the front of the class (make sure the two students come from opposite sides of the room so that they do not already know which objects the other has circled).
The pupils take it in turns to ask a question: *Have you got (a cupboard)?*
The other student replies with a short answer. The first to guess all his/her classmate's objects is the winner. Afterwards, all the pupils do the activity in pairs. In the meantime, walk around the classroom checking on the pronunciation of the questions and answers.

3. Listen and write (p. 29)
Tell the students to turn to page 29 and to look at the first speech bubbles containing the structures used in the exercise. Tell them to observe the spelling, particularly the contracted form *haven't*. Play the cassette once. When they have heard the tape a first time, tell the pupils to cover the speech bubbles at the top of the page. While they listen to the tape a second time the children have to fill in the other speech bubbles.
Play the tape a third time so that the children can fill in any gaps.

Tapescript:

Have you got a skateboard?	*Yes, I have.*
	No, I haven't.
Have you got a television?	*Yes, I have.*
Have you got a computer?	*No, I haven't.*
Have you got a telephone?	*Yes, I have.*
Have you got a cat?	*No, I haven't.*
Have you got a windsurf?	*Yes, I have.*

The pupils check the spelling with the structures in the speech bubbles at the top of the page.

V. HOMEWORK

1. What's there? (p. 28)
The pupils have to make a list of the furniture in each room, as in the example.

2. Draw Peter's funny house
Tell the pupils to draw any two rooms they think might be in Peter's house containing some furniture which is in the wrong place.
Tell them to draw the rooms on a sheet of paper accompanied by a written description.

Lesson 3 pages 30-31

Functions: describing what there is in a place; expressing position
Vocabulary: *box, frogs, everywhere*

I. WARM-UP

Get the children to sing the chant of the verb *to have,* first in the affermative form (re: U4.L1.III,1), then in the interrogative form. As far as the negative form is concerned choose between the following two versions:

- *without got*
- *with got:*

I haven't got, I haven't got
You haven't got, you haven't got
He hasn't got
She hasn't got
We haven't got
You haven't got
They haven't got.

II. CHECKING HOMEWORK

1. What's there? (p. 28)
In order to correct the exercise, ask one child to read out his/her description.
The other pupils swap exercise books to check one another's spelling.

2. Draw Peter's funny house
Ask one member of the class to read out his/her description of Peter's house and to show the class the drawing. Get the pupils to choose the best pictures to be stuck on the wall.

III. CONSOLIDATION

1. Role-play

Ask four pupils to take the parts of Peter, Helen, David and Floppy. To make the activity more theatrical you could get another four students, with their books open at page 26, to stand behind the "actors" and to prompt if necessary. Give the indications in L1:

- Peter invites his friends to go home.
- Helen asks if it is far.
- Peter says that it isn't and that it is right here.
- Helen is surprised and asks where it is.
- Peter points at the house and says that it is up in the tree.
- David expresses his admiration at the tree house.
- Peter invites his friends to go up the ladder.
- Helen encourages Floppy and tells him not to be afraid.
- Peter tells Floppy to come up the ladder. When he sees Floppy hesitating, Peter says that he has an idea.
- While Floppy is being pulled up with a rope, he thinks that he doesn't like Neverland.

2. Freer role-play

Ask two pupils to do carry out a role-play in which they express themselves in English according to the instructions given in L1.
Introduce the situation saying that one pupil will take the part of a foreign child on holiday in England. He/She is playing in the park when he/she meets an English child:

F: *Foreign child*
E: *English child*

F: Say hello to the English child.
E: Reply to the greeting.
F: Ask what time it is.
E: Say that it is five o'clock.
F: Introduce yourself and ask what the other child's name is.
E: Answer and ask where he/she is from.
F: Say that you come from the capital city of your country (give the name of the capital). Ask the English child the same question.
E: Say that you come from Brighton.
F: Say that your mother is over there. Say goodbye.
E: Say goodbye.

This type of role-play is a good way to revise numerous structures. You can modify or enrich the activity according to your purpose.

IV. REVISION

1. The object hunt

As a revision of prepositions of place take a classroom object (*pen, pencil-case, ruler,* etc.) and ask one pupil to go out of the room while you hide the object. With the help of the other students write on the blackboard where the object is, for example:
It's under the teacher's desk.
Tell the pupil to come back into the classroom and to find the object on the basis of what is written on the blackboard. The next time, the same pupil asks another member of the class to leave the classroom while he/she hides an object and writes where it is to be found on the blackboard with your help.
Try to guide the game so that all the prepositions that have been introduced so far are revised.

2. Test a friend

Divide the blackboard into two parts: on one side write OBJECTS at the top with a list of objects underneath (for example: *lamp, book, flowers, yoghurt, T-shirt,* etc.); on the other side write PLACES at the top with a list of places where these objects can be found below (for example: *fridge, garden, table, desk, wardrobe*, etc.).

In pairs, the pupils ask and answer questions as follows:
Where's the ...?/Where are the ...?
It's/they're on/in/under/near the ...
to establish realistic positions.
Allow the children ten minutes to complete the mini-dialogues and to write them in their exercise books. Proceed with the correction once everybody has finished.

V. PRACTICE

1. Look and write (p. 30)
Tell the students to open their books at page 30 and to look at the pictures carefully. Read out the first example, then ask one pupil to complete the sentence beneath the second illustration. Give the children some time to finish the remaining sentences.
Once the activity has been completed, you could get the children to read out the sentences with a rap rhythm:
On an island there's a wood.
In the wood there's a house (cottage).
In the house (cottage) there's a bedroom.
In the bedroom there's a wardrobe.
In the wardrobe there's a box.
In the box there's a dog (Floppy).

VI. LET'S SING A SONG

1. Close your eyes and listen
Tell the children to close their eyes while they listen to the song "*Frogs everywhere*" and to concentrate on the sounds they hear.

2. Look and listen
Get the students to open their books at page 31 and listen to the song as they read the words.
Once they have heard the song twice the children should be able to say where the sixth frog is. (*Under the sofa*).

3. Mime the words
The pupils pretend to sing the song by moving only their lips without producing any sounds.

4. Let's sing
The children sing the song all together.

VII. HOMEWORK

1. In a forest there's a ...
Write the above phrase on the blackboard and tell the pupils to copy it into their exercise books. The children create a short story as in the example on page 30 for homework. Stimulate them to imagine what there could be in a forest by talking about it in L1 in class. The children have to illustrate the story too.

2. Write your own song
On the basis of the song "*Frogs everywhere*" ask the pupils to make up a new version of the song by substituting frogs with another animal, an object or a food and by introducing other reference points. You could suggest the following version as an example:
Sugar, sugar everywhere:
on the table,
on the sofa,
in the cupboard,
near the window,
on the floor
and ... where more?
During the next lesson the pupils could choose the most original version and copy it on a sheet of paper to be stuck on the wall in the classroom.

Unit 5 - Going shopping

Lesson 1 pages 32-33

Functions: expressing a need
Structures: *I need a/an/some ...*
Vocabulary: *something, baker's, bread, greengrocer's, everything, toothpaste, toothbrush, chemist, funny, shoes, a pair of ...*

I. WARM-UP

1. Sing the song
Get the children to sing the song "*Frogs everywhere*" all together, then ask a volunteer to sing it in front of the class.

II. CHECKING HOMEWORK

1. In the forest there's a ...
Tell the pupils to work in pairs to compare their new texts.
In the meantime walk around the classroom providing assistance if necessary.
Afterwards, ask each child to read out his/her version and to show the rest of the class his/her picture.
It is important to encourage the pupils' individual creativity and to make them feel proud of their ability to express themselves in a foreign language.

2. Sing your own song
Ask some of the children to sing their version of the song to the rest of the class.
The pupils judge which song they like the most.
At the end of the "musical contest" everybody sings the favourite song together.

III. PRESENTATION: Going shopping

1. Look and answer

Tell the children to open their books at pages 32 and 33 and to look at the illustrations carefully.
Then ask them in L1:

- Where is Peter going with David, Helen and Floppy?
- Are the shops like the ones where you live?
- What differences can you see?
- What's happening in the last picture?

Ask some questions in English after having told the students to number the pictures from 1 to 11:

- *Who can you see in picture number 1?*
- *Is Pit in picture number 4?*
- *Is Peter happy or sad in picture number 4?*
- *Is Peter holding apples and bananas in picture number 6?*
- *How many T-shirts can you count in picture number 9?*
- *What colour are they?*

2. Close your eyes and listen

Tell the pupils to close their eyes while they listen to the dialogue. Afterwards, ask them which words or phrases struck them most.

3. Mime the words

With their books open the students follow the dialogue and pretend to be the characters who are speaking by moving their lips without producing any sounds.

4. Listen and repeat

Check that everybody has understood the dialogue, particularly the structure:
Where are you going?
I'm going to buy ...
and the expressions *baker's* and *greengrocer's*. Then get the children to listen to the cassette again and to repeat after each phrase.

IV. PRACTICE

1. I need some ..., I need a/an ...

Point out the structure *I need* and ask the students to find all the affermative sentences in the dialogue with this structure (*I need some toothpaste and a toothbrush. I need a new pair of jeans and a new pair of shoes*).
Provide other examples of expressions with *I need* such as:
I need some bananas.
I need some bread.
I need a pair of shoes.
I need an exercise book.
Get the students to repeat one of the model phrases but to choose another noun.

2. Shopping list

Ask the pupils to make a list of products in English that usually appear on a shopping list such as:
tomatoes, potatoes, bread, milk...
The list could be made by asking questions:
What can you buy for dinner/lunch/breakfast?
to which each pupil answers:
I can buy a/an/some ...
Write the noun preceded by the article or by *some* on the blackboard.
Then tell each pupil to write the name of a food on a piece of paper, without showing it to his/her classmates.
Prepare a shopping list including 5 of the products named earlier.
Give the list to one child who has to ask the other pupils for the products using the following phrases:
Excuse me, I need a/an/some (coke).
Have you got any?
If the pupil has that product, he/she replies:
Yes, I have. Here you are.
If not, he/she answers:
No, I'm sorry. I haven't.
Once the child has had 5 turns at guessing who has got those products, the list is passed to another pupil whose turn it is to try and guess.

3. A Poster: Shops and goods

During this lesson you could take the opportunity to extend the vocabulary relating to the goods on sale in the various shops mentioned in the unit.

You could get the pupils to design a poster divided into different columns with each column assigned to one type of shop.

Tell the children to stick newspaper or magazine cuttings relating to the goods on sale in each type of shop onto the poster.

With your help or with a bilingual dictionary, the children have to write the name of the product in English beneath the picture.

This poster will be useful when preparing mini-dialogues on the subject.

V. HOMEWORK

1. Read the dialogue (p. 32-33)

Tell the children to read the dialogue at home so that they will be prepared to act it out in class during the next lesson.

Lesson 2 pages 34-35

Functions: asking what somebody needs
Structures: *What do you need?*
Vocabulary: *book shop, pet shop, supermarket, shoe shop, record shop, clothes shop, greengrocer, toy shop, baker, lead, cassette*

I. CHECKING HOMEWORK

1. Act the dialogue (p. 32-33)
Ask three volunteers to act out the dialogue in front of the class. Make sure they use suitable gestures and that their intonation is correct.

II. CONSOLIDATION

1. Role-play
Propose a guided role-play on the basis of the dialogue introduced in the previous lesson. This activity will help the pupils to understand and remember the structures and expressions.
Ask three or four pupils to be either themselves or children of different nationalities (in the latter case, let them choose their names). Once the various roles have been decided, tell the children to follow the indications you give them in L1.
For example, you could use the following sequence:
- (Paul and John) meet (Mary) and ask her where she is going.
- (Mary) says that she is hungry and that she is going to buy something to eat.

- (John) says that he is hungry too.
- (Mary) suggests they go to the baker's.
- (Mary and John) agree.
- Then (Mary) tells her friends that she wants to go to the greengrocer's because she needs some oranges.
- (Paul) says that he needs a toothbrush and some toothpaste and asks where the chemist is.
- (Mary) shows him where it is.
- (Paul) thanks (Mary) and says goodbye.

You will probably need to remind the students of the expressions the first time they perform the role-play.
If this is the case, repeat the activity with another group of pupils.

III. PRESENTATION AND PRACTICE: Shops

1. Look, listen and touch (p. 34-35)
Play the section on tape where the different shops are named at random. The pupils have to touch the respective illustration.

2. What do they need? Where do they go? (p. 34-35)
Ask one child to read out what David says and another Peter's reply.
Explain that the pupils have to fill in the empty speech bubbles expressing what each person needs on the basis of the picture. The pupils use the structure:
I need a/an/some ...
Peter Pan then tells each child to go to the right shop using the structure:
Go to the ...!
Once all the students have participated in the activity get them to complete the speech bubbles while you walk around the classroom.
Example:
- *I need a new lead.*
  Go to the pet shop!
- *I need a new pair of shoes.*
  Go to the shoe shop!
- *I need some orange juice.*
  Go to the supermarket!
- *I need a new book.*
  Go to the book shop!
- *I need some bread.*
  Go to the baker's!
- *I need a new pair of jeans.*
  Go to the clothes shop!
- *I need some fruit.*
  Go to the greengrocer's!
- *I need a new doll.*
  Go to the toy shop!
- *I need a new cassette.*
  Go to the record shop!

IV. PRESENTATION: Asking and giving prices

1. How much is it? It's ...
How much are they? They're ...
Take a pen and show the class a label with the price: 40p. Explain that p stands for pence, which is one hundredth of one pound (£).
Then say:
How much is the pen?
Look. It's 40p.
Provide other examples:

a ruler	*70p*
a pencil	*25p*
an exercise-book	*£1*
a book	*£15*

Afterwards, hold up more than one object saying:
How much are the pens?
They're 40p each.

V. REMEMBER

Once the children have understood how to ask the price, put the two examples on the blackboard and tell the children to copy them into their exercise books under the heading: *Remember!*

VI. PRACTICE

1. At the greengrocer's

On the blackboard draw a greengrocer's counter with some fruit and the respective prices, for example:

Apples *60p a kilo*
Bananas *80p a kilo*
Lemons *35p / each*
Tomatoes *50p a kilo*
Potatoes *25p a kilo*

Together with the pupils make up a mini-dialogue between a shopkeeper and a customer.

The dialogue could proceed as follows:

C: Good morning!
S: Good morning!
C: I need a kilo of apples.
S: Here you are!
C: How much are they?
S: 60p
C: Thank you!
S: Good-bye
C: Good-bye

If you consider it the case, write the dialogue on the blackboard and get the pupils to copy it into their exercise books. It could be useful as a model for other mini-dialogues.

VII. HOMEWORK

1. What do they need? Where do they go? (p.34-35)

To consolidate the structures tell the children to copy what the characters in the textbook say and Peter Pan's response.

2. Write mini-dialogues

The children have to make up two mini-dialogues for two different shops like the one practised during the lesson.

3. Break the code and find the message (p.34)

The pupils have to break the code to find out what Floppy is thinking on page 34.

Lesson 3 pages 36-37

Listen and write

Who's going to the baker's?
Who's going to the supermarket?
Who's going to the pet shop?
Who's going to the record shop?
Who's going to the greengrocer's?
Who's going to the book shop?
Who's going to the toy shop?
Who's going to the clothes shop?

36

Let's sing!

Eat a cake!
I'm eating a cake.
Yum... Yum...

Drink a coke!
I'm drinking a coke.
Glug... glug...

Clap your hands!
I'm clapping my hands.
Clap.... clap...

Stamp your feet!
I'm stamping my feet.
Stamp... stamp...

Now stop it!
Just sit down!
We're all sitting down.

37

Functions: talking about an action that is taking place
Structures: *I'm (V-ing). Who's (V-ing)?*

I. CHECKING HOMEWORK

1. What do you need? Where do they go? (p. 34-35)
Walk around the classroom checking that everyone has done the exercise correctly.

2. Write mini-dialogues
Ask one pupil to read out his/her dialogue prepared at home, getting the child's deskmate to take the part of either the customer or the shopkeeper. Walk around the room checking that the spelling is correct.

3. Break the code and find the message (p. 34)
Ask one member of the class to read out his/her solution and to explain the meaning in L1.
Tell the students to advise Floppy as to where he should go to buy some dog food using the structure that Peter uses on the same page.
(*Floppy: I'm hungry. Can I have some dog food? Go to the supermarket/pet shop!*).

II. CONSOLIDATION

1. Freer role-play
Ask two volunteers to come up to the front of the class to follow the instructions given in L1 and to express themselves in English. The two pupils take the part of a customer

and a shopkeeper: they could pretend that your desk is the counter.
The scene could take place in a clothes shop, so write on the board:
At the clothes shop.
Add useful expressions such as:
Which size?
Small/medium/large/extra large
to ask and say what size you need.
What colour do you like?
to ask for information about colour.
The pupils have to demonstrate their ability to use the structures they know by expressing themselves in L2 according to the following indications:

C: *customer*
S: *shopkeeper*

C: Enter the shop saying good morning.
S: Reply.
C: Say that you need a pink T-shirt.
S: Ask what size the customer takes.
C: Answer that you need a medium-sized one.
S: Say that you do not have a medium, but a large one.
C: Say that it's alright.
S: Give the T-shirt to the customer.
C: Thank the shopkeeper and ask how much it costs.
S: Say that it costs £25.
C: Hand the shopkeeper the money, thank him/her and say goodbye.
S: Thank the customer and say goodbye.

You could get other students to repeat the role-play changing the colour of the T-shirt, the size, the cost or even the article.

III. PRACTICE

1. Chain game
Repeat the exchange of words between David and Peter Pan in the first picture of the dialogue on page 32:

David: *Where are you going, Peter?*
Peter: *I'm hungry. I'm going to buy something to eat.*
Start the "chain" by asking one child the question to which he/she replies:
- *I'm hungry. I'm going to buy a/an/some (food).*

2. Listen and write (p. 36)
Tell the pupils to open their books at page 36 and to look at the objects the characters are holding that suggest what they need.
Play the tape once.
The students write down the phrases in the speech bubbles the second time they hear the cassette.
The third time you play the tape, the children check what they have written.

Tapescript:

- *I need some fruit.*
- *I'm going to buy a new book.*
- *I'm going to buy a new lead.*
- *I need a new cassette.*
- *I'm going to buy a new doll.*
- *I need a new pair of shoes.*
- *I need some bread.*
- *I'm going to buy a new pair of jeans.*
- *I need some orange juice.*

3. Give suggestions
Read out the speech bubbles one at a time. The pupils have to suggest which shop to go to using *Go to the ...*

4. Who's going where? (p. 36)
The children have to answer the questions on page 36 orally by saying who is performing the action as in the example:
Who's going to the baker's?
Pit is going to the baker's.
You could get the students to use a rap rhythm for the exchange of words.

IV. THINK

Once the pupils have practised the form *am/is going*, write a model phrase on the blackboard, for example:
I'm going to the book shop.
Get the children to work out the forms for the remaining subjects on the basis of their knowledge of the verb *to be*.
Write all the forms on the board for reference.

V. REMEMBER

The pupils read aloud what is written on the blackboard and copy down the verb forms in their exercise books under the heading: *Remember!*

VI. LET'S SING A SONG

1. "Eat a cake" (p. 37)
Introduce the song and explain that the pupils will come across other examples of the verb forms practised previously.

2. Close your eyes and listen
Tell the children to close their eyes as they listen to the song. Afterwards, ask them if they recognised any of the words.

3. Look and listen
The pupils listen to the song once again and follow the text in their books.

4. Listen and mime
Get the children to stand up and mime the song as they hear it again.

5. Mime the words
The pupils pretend to sing the song by moving their lips without producing any sounds.

6. Let's sing
At this stage get the class to sing the song together miming the various actions.

VII. HOMEWORK

1. Learn the song by heart
The children have to learn the song by heart.

Once you have completed the first five units, it is advisable to consolidate what has been introduced up to now so that all the pupils reach the same level. Both the revision game (pages 38-39) in the book and the other revision activities presented here provide stimulating and interesting consolidation exercises which can be useful for a few lessons before testing your students.

REVISION GAME

Materials: 1 dice and a marker for each pupil
Purpose: consolidation of language regarding commands, numbers, days of the week, months, seasons, members of the family, parts of the body, food, actions.

The game is played in pairs. Each pupil will try to beat his/her partner to the finish. Explain that each child must have a marker (a rubber, a pen top, a pencil sharpener or a small piece of paper etc..) and that it will be moved along according to the number obtained when the dice is thrown.
Whoever reaches the finish first is the winner.
Clarify some of the terms needed to play the game correctly such as, *if* and *go back to*. Point out that the children must speak in English throughout the game especially when they read out the number obtained when they throw the dice. If anyone speaks in L1 then they miss a turn.
After having read the phrase in the space they land on, the pupils must reply in English. For example, if someone lands on stone number one with:
If your birthday's in winter, go to 5. If not, go to 7.
He/She must answer:
Yes, my birthday's in winter.
Or:
No, my birthday's not in winter. It's in summer.
Walk around the classroom while the children are playing the game checking that they are sticking to the rules and that L2 is being used.

TEN MORE REVISION ACTIVITIES

1. TALL OR SMALL?

Purpose: consolidation of vocabulary relating to the body.

Tell the children to listen to the following nursery rhyme accompanied by some appropriate gestures. Get the pupils to do the movements too:

Sometimes we're very, very short,
(everybody bends down)
Sometimes we're very, very tall,
(everybody stands on tiptoe with their arms stretched up towards the ceiling)
Close your eyes and turn around
and guess which we're now.

Ask a volunteer to come to the front of the class and to perform the gestures as the rest of the class recite the rhyme.
The volunteer closes his/her eyes and turns around and then guesses which position his/her classmates are miming:

Now you're short/tall!

Each pupil has one go, after which he/she has to choose another person to take his/her place.
However, if the student does not guess the position, then he/she has to do a little forfeit.
At the end of the game, you could let the children copy the nursery rhyme into their exercise books so that it can be used if

they want to play the game on other occasions.

2. A SONG: "THIS IS THE WAY ..."

Purpose: consolidation of vocabulary relating to parts of the body; revision of days of the week.

To the traditional tune of "*Here we go round the mulberry bush*" teach the children the following song and mime the actions mentioned:

This is the way I wash my face
wash my face, wash my face,
This is the way I wash my face
on Monday morning.

This is the way I brush my teeth, ...
on Tuesday morning.

This is the way I comb my hair, ...
on Wednesday morning.

This is the way I clap my hands, ...
on Thursday morning.

This is the way I cross my arms, ...
on Friday morning.

This is the way I close my eyes, ...
on Saturday morning.

This is the way I stamp my feet, ...
on Sunday morning.

First introduce the song orally accompanied by the movements and get the children to perform the gestures.
Once the pupils feel confident with the song write the words on the blackboard to consolidate comprehension and pronunciation.
Tell the students to copy the words of the song into their exercise books.

3. A LETTER TO A PEN-FRIEND

Purpose: presenting yourself and description of physical appearance.

You could give the class the outline of a simple letter to be sent either to an imaginary or a real friend who will reply in English. This will give the children the chance to present themselves, to describe themselves, their families and where they live, and to speak about what they like and what they do not like.
The outline of the letter to be written on the board could be as follows:

Dear (name),

My name's ..., I'm a/an (nationality) (boy/girl) and I'm (age).
I'm ... and ...; I've got ... and ... (physical description).
I live in a (house/flat) with my family: (members of family).
My (sister/brother)'s name is .... She/he is (age).
She/He's got (physical description). We've got a (pet), (name).
I like ..., but I don't like ... (food, colours, sport).
Please write back soon.
Yours (name).

The pupils write the letter in their exercise books filling in the spaces with their personal details.
If the letter is to be sent to a foreign pen-friend then it must be written on a separate sheet of paper.
When the reply arrives get the pupil to stick it into his/her exercise book next to the original letter.
Help the children to understand the reply from the foreign student.
If you don't plan to start up an exchange of letters between your pupils and students

from other countries, you could get the children to exchange letters amongst themselves and to write a reply to the letter they have received, so they have two letters in their exercise books.

4. CATEGORY BOUNCE

Materials: a dice; a ball; numbered pieces of paper; a sheet of paper containing six tasks for each category.
Purpose: consolidation of vocabulary relating to different categories; revision of structures such as the verb *to be, to have, to like, can.*

The test sheets must be prepared beforehand either by you at home or in class with the pupils working together in small groups.
For example, the six tasks for the category Countries and nationalities could be:
1. Name five countries.
2. Ask where your friend comes from.
3. Say that Mary comes from France.
4. Say that you are an Italian boy/girl.
5. Say the name of a country with six letters (if the alphabet has been done, you could ask the spelling of a country).
6. Say that the capital of Spain is Madrid.

Before starting the game, draw a table on the blackboard containing 6 to 10 squares, according to the categories that you wish to revise (*countries and nationalities, toys, months, shops, animals,* etc.). Each square should be numbered and contain a category.

1 TOYS	2 MONTHS	3 SHOPS
4 ANIMALS	5 COUNTRIES	6 FOOD

Prepare some small pieces of paper (the number will depend on the number of squares in the table) each of which will be numbered and folded up.
The pupils play the game in groups of three (make sure the groups are as homogeneous as possible with regard to linguistic and practical ability). Each group will be called out in turns to come up to your desk and to extract a small piece of paper with a number which represents the category they have to concentrate on.
Then one child throws the dice and calls out the number he/she gets.
Look at the test sheet and read out the task which corresponds to the number on the dice.
In the meantime the child starts to bounce the ball. If he/she drops the ball before he/she finishes the task, or if he/she answers wrongly, then another member of the group has to try.
If he/she fails too then it is the third person's turn and so on until the right answer is obtained.
Make note of the number of times the ball changes hands before the task is performed correctly.
Then another group has a go.
After two turns for each group, the winning team is the one that passes the ball from one member to another the least number of times.

5. MY HOUSE

Purpose: consolidation of vocabulary relating to the house.

Each pupil has to draw a plan of his/her house seen from above (one for each floor if necessary). The name of each room has to be written in English and three pieces of furniture must be mentioned in L2.
Write the following sentences on the board which the pupils have to copy into their exercise books and complete:

In my house I've got (number) rooms: (name of the rooms).
In the (name of one room) there is (furniture).
Tell the pupils to use adjectives such as: *old/new, big/small, comfortable, beautiful, nice,* as well as adjectives of colour.
Afterwards, the children take it in turns to read out their descriptions.

6. BIRDS EVERYWHERE

Purpose: consolidation of prepositions and vocabulary relating to the classsroom.

With reference to the song in Unit 4 ask the children to draw the objects according to the following instructions:

Draw a desk.
Draw a book on the desk.
Draw a pencil case near the book.
Draw a chair under the desk.
Draw a school-bag near the chair.

Then tell the children to draw some birds according to the suggestions:

One bird is under the desk.
One bird is on the book.
One bird is near the pencil case.
One bird is on the chair.
One bird is in the school-bag.

Read out the text once again so that the pupils can check their pictures.
Then ask one child to show the class his/her drawing.

7. WHERE ARE YOU GOING?

Purpose: consolidation of the names of shops, vocabulary relating to food, toys and clothes etc.

Start up a short conversation between one pupil and the rest of the class, for example:
pupil (going towards the door):
Bye-bye everybody.
Class: *Where are you going?*
Pupil: *I'm going to the (shop).*
Class: *Why?*
Pupil: *Guess.*
Class: *To buy a/an/some/ ...*
Each time, before starting the activity, the pupil must whisper to you what he/she wants to buy.
The first person to give the right answer continues the game.

8. SHOPPING CHAIN

Purpose: consolidation of vocabulary relating to shops and goods; consolidation of pronunciation.

Introduce the game by saying that each pupil has to repeat what his/her classmate has said and to add another item that can be purchased from the shop that has been named.
Whoever makes a mistake in repeating or in adding another good has to do a small forfeit.
Start off the game by saying:
I'm going to the supermarket to buy some chips.
The choice of the supermarket obviously enables the children to name a variety of products.
Then point at the child who has to continue the game by repeating the phrase and adding something else to buy.
Make sure the students pay attention to their use of the article.
If somebody forgets the exact order of the goods or makes a mistake in the pronunciation the game starts again.

9. THE SHOPPING BAG

Purpose: consolidation of the vocabulary relating to shopping.

Tell the children to open their exercise books and to draw a picture of a transparent shopping bag so that you can see the contents. Get each pupil to draw five purchases in the bag, making sure that the other members of the class can not see the picture.
The students play the game in pairs and have five goes to guess at least three of the five articles asking:
Have you got a/an/any ...?
The partner answers:
Yes, I have or *Sorry, I haven't.*
Each pupil must note down the things mentioned on a piece of paper so as not to repeat them later on. After the first five questions, it is the other child's turn to guess what it is in his/her partner's bag. Alternate in this way, until the first person manages to guess at least three of the items in the other's shopping bag. He/she is the winner.

10. DRAMA

Purpose: to consolidate the structures introduced in the first five units of the book.

Tell the pupils to act out the adventures of the characters in *Magic!* in the first five units.
Choose different children to take the part of the characters in the book for each unit. Those pupils who do not act out the dialogues could sing the songs presented in the five units either individually or in groups.
In this way, the lesson will be somewhat different, rather like a little show. Make sure that the children who are acting or singing have the audience, made up of the other members of the class, in front of them. Suggest the pupils dress up to make the show all the more theatrical.

TEST 1

NAME .... MARK ....

1. Listen and fill in the gaps:

Hello! My .... is Andrew Smith.
I'm .... years old and I'm ....
I'm .... and thin. ...'.... got green .... and .... hair.
I .... in a flat in .... with my ...., ... and ....
My sister's .... is Susan. She's .... and she's .... nice.
We've got a pet. It's .... dog called Blacky.
Dogs ...... my favourite ....

2. Give the right suggestions:

- I need some milk.
  Go to the ....
- I need a pink T-shirt.
  ....
- I need a new school-bag.
  ....
- I need some fruit.
  ....
- I need a new skateboard.
  ....
- I need a big kennel for my dog.
  ....

3. Check in your book and find out:

a. Is Sammy tall?

....

b. Where's Teddy from?

....

c. Who's from France?

....

d. What colour are Hook's eyes?

....

e. Who's Smythe?

....

f. What's there in Peter's house?

....

4. Draw a kitchen and describe it:

In this kitchen ....
....
....
....
....

TEST 1 - NOTES FOR THE TEACHER

The **first exercise** in test number 1 aims at testing the listening, comprehension and writing skills. Read out the text:
Hello! My name is Andrew Smith. I'm nine years old and I'm English. I'm tall and thin. I've got green eyes and blond hair.
I live in a flat in London with my mum, my dad and my sister.
My sister's name is Susan. She's five and she's very nice.
We've got a pet. It's a dog called Blacky.
Dogs are my favourite animals.
The missing words are underlined and the pupils have to insert them correctly. You could pause when you read out these words or read the text twice to enable the children to complete it.
The **second exercise** aims at stimulating the ability to read individually and understand a short sentence and give some advise in L2.
The **third exercise** is an activity based on comprehension of the textbook and formulation of the right answer using structures that have been presented.
The **fourth exercise** is a free composition revising vocabulary and structures already introduced and it tests the pupils' ability to write a description in L2.

CORRECTION OF TEST NUMBER 1

The correction of the test should take place in class during the following lesson and should involve all the students.
Distribute the test sheets making sure that each pupil receives someone else's test and not his/her own.
This will stimulate the pupils to pay attention while you guide them in their correction of another person's test.
First of all, read out the text in the **first exercise** and then write either all of it on the blackboard or only the missing words. If any words have been written wrongly or if they are missing altogether tell the children to write in the correct ones with a red pen without crossing out the wrong version.
Ask one pupil to read out the suggestions in the **second exercise** while the others listen out for mistakes.
Correct the **third exercise** in the same way, by getting the children to participate actively either from their desks or by asking them to take it in turns to write the correct answers on the board.
If there are any mistakes tell the students to correct them by writing the correct answer above the error without rubbing it out.
Since the **fourth exercise** is a composition, check each pupil's version before the lesson as individual correction is necessary.
You could however ask a child to read out his/her composition in class and use it to do a picture dictation: as the pupil reads it out the other members of the class draw the kitchen being described.
When the correction phase has finished, write your marking criteria on the blackboard. By counting the number of mistakes, the pupils will put the relative mark in the space provided on the test sheet. The students then give you back the test sheets. After looking at the tests briefly, note down the marks and give each sheet back to the person who did the test.
The pupils make a note of their mistakes and, if necessary, tell them to write out the wrong word a number of times in their exercise books in order to remind them of the correct spelling.
Each pupil must take the test sheet home and ask one of his/her parents to sign it. The following lesson the test sheets are returned to you.

Unit 6 - Magic in Neverland

Lesson 1 pages 40-41

Functions: expressing ability
Structures: *They can ...*
Vocabulary: *around, fly, sing, jump, dance, dangerous*
Phonology: /ŋ /

I. WARM-UP

1. Sing the song
Tell the children to sing the song "*Eat a cake*" on page 37, accompanied by suitable gestures.

II. PRESENTATION: Present Continuous

1. Read and underline
Tell the children to underline the imperative and *-ing* verb forms in the song. Ask one pupil to read out the words that he/she has underlined. Check the pronunciation of /ŋ / in the ending *-ing*.
Then get the students to look carefully at the variation in the written form of some verbs in changing from the imperative to the continuous form (*clap-clapping, sit-sitting*).

2. Copy in the right column
Tell the children to open their exercise books so they have two white pages in front of them.
Get them to divide each page into two columns, the first one for the imperative and the second for the *-ing* form.

On the left-hand page the pupils write the verbs in the song that form the gerund by adding simply *-ing*.
On the other page, they write the verbs with a variation in the written form (underlined in red).
If you consider it the case, beneath each verb write the equivalent in L1.
Explain to the students that, from now on, all the verb forms they come across should be noted in their exercise books in the appropriate columns. Tell the children to reread the dialogue in *Unit 5* and to add the verb that appears (*go-going*).

III. THINK

Try to encourage the students, when they see a verb with a variation in the *-ing* form, to work out the doubling rule: with monosyllabic verbs which end with one consonant preceded by only one vowel.
Before reading the *-ing* form of the verbs in the two lists, ask the pupils to pay attention to pronunciation and to say whether they notice any obvious differences.
The children will have no difficulty in recognising that the double consonant does not produce any change in pronunciation.

IV. PRACTICE

1. The deaf game
Briefly revise the vocabulary relating to actions such as: *open, close, write, read, listen, draw, clap, stamp, eat, drink,* etc. and get the pupils to mime the verbs.
Ask one child quietly:
What are you doing?
The child has to pretend that he/she can not hear what you have said and asks: *What?*
The rest of the class ask the question all together:
What are you doing?
At this stage, the pupil replies, for example:
I'm reading.

2. A guessing game
Ask two students to come up to the front of the class.
One of them has to mime an action (for example: walking) after having told his/her partner what he/she is doing.
The second pupil refers to the class what the other is doing.
Ask: *Are you (walking)?*
The pupil answers: *Yes, I am.*
Afterwards, get the other members of the class to ask the questions.
Once the structure has been assimilated tell the child who is referring what the other is doing, along with two or three other pupils to stand in front of the child who is miming the actions so that the rest of the class can not see him/her. The other members of the class take it in turns to ask questions in order to guess the action that is being mimed.
You could also get the children to practise the third person singular. In this case, they ask the pupils forming "the wall":
Is he/she (writing)?

V. PRESENTATION: Magic in Neverland

1. Look and answer
Tell the children to open their books at pages 40 and 41 and to look at the pictures carefully. Then ask in L1:
- What's happening in Neverland?
- What strange things are the animals doing?
- Why can they do such unusual things?
- Why is Floppy afraid in the last picture?

2. Close your eyes and listen
Tell the children to close their eyes and to concentrate on what they hear while they listen to the dialogue.
Afterwards, ask them which words or phrases struck them most.

3. Mime the words
The pupils follow the dialogue with their books open and pretend to be the characters in the story by moving their lips without producing any sounds.

4. Listen and repeat
Check that everybody has understood the dialogue and ask the students to repeat after each phrase.

VI. HOMEWORK

1. Read the dialogue (p. 40-41)
The pupils have to read the dialogue so that they will be prepared to act it out during the next lesson.

Lesson 2 pages 42-43

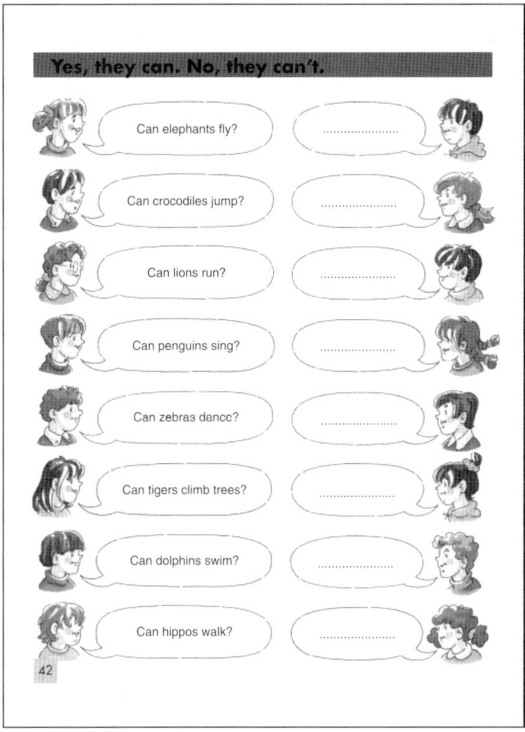

Functions: expressing an ability in the interrogative and negative forms; short answers; demonstrative pronouns
Structures: *Can elephants fly? Yes, they can/No, they can't. These/those*
Vocabulary: *penguins, zebras, dolphins*

I. CHECKING HOMEWORK

1. Act the dialogue (p. 40-41)

Ask a few volunteers to act out the dialogue in front of the rest of the class. Let them use their books if they wish.
Check that their gestures are appropriate and the intonation is correct.

II. PRESENTATION

1. I can/ I can't

In order to introduce the interrogative form, ask one child:
Can you fly?
The pupil will probably reply only:
Yes!/No!
Point out that, even though the answer is sufficient, in many situations the English usually reply saying:
Yes, I can!
No, I can't!
Take care to prolong the pronunciation of the "a" in the negative form.
To practise the correct pronunciation of *I can* and *I can't* write the words on two sheets of paper.
As you alternate the words *can* and *can't* quickly hold up the respective sheet of

paper. Make the rhythm quite rapid to make it sound like the noise of a train.
I can. I can't.
I can. I can't.
I can. I can't.

III. PRACTICE

1. Can you sing?
Walk around the classroom asking the children:
Can you sing?
Can you jump?
Can you dance?
Can you touch your toes without bending your knees?
Can you touch your knee with your nose?
Can you touch your nose with your tongue?
The pupils reply with short answers.

2. Yes, they can. No, they can't. (p. 42)
Ask the pupils to open their books at page 42.
Read out the phrases in the speech bubbles getting the children to reply using the suitable short answer.
If the pupils give an affermative answer to the question *Can penguins sing?* point out that, even though penguins belong to the bird family, the sound they emit can not strictly be defined as a "song".
Thanks to this sound the penguins can leave the other members of their group to go and look for food and then find them again amongst the multitude of penguins.

3. Write the verbs in the right columns
Tell the pupils to put the verbs they have come across on page 42 in their exercise books as indicated in U6.L1.II,2.
Check this activity by asking one pupil to come up to the blackboard and to write down the verbs inserted in the columns on each page.

IV. PRESENTATION

1. These and those
To introduce the plural form of the demonstrative pronouns, put some pens on your desk, and some books on a desk at the back of the classroom.
Then point at a pen saying:
This is my pen,
highlighting the pronoun *this* with your voice.
Afterwards point at the group of pens on your desk and say:
These are my pens,
stressing *these* and *pens* with your voice, to highlight the plural forms. In the same way, introduce the plural of *that*, by first pointing at a book and then at the pile of books at the back of the classroom.

V. PRACTICE

1. Move and say: What are these? What are those?
To help the children remember the demonstrative pronouns, suggest the following rhyme which will be very stimulating if the pupils take off their shoes and socks and sit on the floor with their legs stretched out in front of them:

What are these?
(showing their fingers)
What are those?
(pointing at their toes)
These are my twiddling fingers.
(moving their fingers)
Those are my twiddling toes.
(pointing at their toes as they move them).

2. Other sentences
Tell the children to look around them and to produce sentences with *these* and *those*, for example:
These are my books.
Those are windows.
These are (Paolo)'s books.

VI. HOMEWORK

1. What are they doing? (p. 43)
Tell the children to open their books at page 43. Ask a volunteer to read out the first speech bubble and point out the position of the penguins with respect to Peter, therefore practising the use of *these*. Then ask another child to read out the second speech bubble, and highlight the distance and therefore the use of *those*. The pupils have to write correct sentences, being careful with the plural form of the verb *to be* and the written form of the verbs in the *-ing* form.

Lesson 3 pages 44-45

Functions: descriptions with colours and numbers
Vocabulary: *sheep, horse, cow, hen, chick*
Phonology: plurals in -es /iz/

I. WARM-UP

1. Answer the questions
Get a few pupils to answer some questions in English relating to the dialogue on pages 40 and 41:

- *Is Helen happy or sad in picture number 2? And Floppy? Is he happy?*
- *How many elephants can you see in picture number 4?*
- *What can elephants do in Neverland?*
- *What animals can you see on page 41?*
- *What can crocodiles do?*
- *What can lions do?*

- *And what can the hippos do?*
- *Is Floppy angry at the end?*

II. CHECKING HOMEWORK

1. What are they doing? Listen and check (p. 43)

Play the cassette to check the exercise and consolidate the pronunciation.

Tapescript:

These penguins are singing.
Those elephants are flying.
These crocodiles are dancing.
Those tigers are climbing trees.
These zebras are singing.
Those dolphins are swimming.
Those lions are running.

Once they have heard the tape ask the pupils whether they can think up alternative actions from the picture. The following could be given:
These penguins are dancing.
These zebras are dancing.
Those dolphins are jumping.

III. CONSOLIDATION

1. What can animals do in Neverland?

Write the following sentences on the blackboard:
Elephants can't fly.
But they can fly in Neverland.
Tell the children to work in pairs to supply further examples using the text of the dialogue on pages 40 and 41.
Ask the pupils to think of unusual actions that other animals might do in Neverland.
Listen to their suggestions and you could write a list of these actions to be hung up in the classroom.

IV. PRESENTATION: A visit to the farm (p. 44)

1. Listen and point

Tell the children to open their books at pages 44 and 45. Play the cassette and get the pupils to point at the animals in the book as they are mentioned.
When Peter Pan says:
Look for a black chick!
the children have to find it (*near the tree*).

2. How many legs altogether (p. 44)

Play the tape at least twice with textbooks closed so the children can answer Old Mac Donald's question. The first time they hear the cassette the pupils write down the number and name of the animals, while the second listening will be used to check what they have written. Tell each child to calculate the total number of legs.
The first to finish calls out the answer.
If the answer is wrong then you could check in more detail by asking:
- *How many legs has one cow got?*
- *So how legs have two cows got?*
- *How many legs has one sheep got?*
- *So how many legs have three sheep got?*
With such questions, the pupils have to think about the singular and plural forms of both the verb and the noun.
Get as many children as possible to participate and each time write the numbers on the board which will be added up at the end giving the correct solution (*60 legs*).

3. Listen and answer

Ask the following question:
What colour are chicks usually? Explain the meaning of *usually* if necessary.
Once the children have answered (*yellow*), repeat the same question for all the other animals on this farm, for example:
What colour are sheep usually?
What colour are horses usually?
What colour are cows usually?

V. THINK

Point out the pronunciation of the plural of *horse*: *horses*. Then ask the children to give the plural of *house*.
With regard to *sheep*, whose plural form remains unchanged, explain that it is an exception to the rule.

VI. PRACTICE

1. Animal chain
Start a chain by asking the question:
What animals can you see?
Each pupil answers the question by adding the number and name of another animal, for example:
Pupil 1: *I can see three sheep.*
Pupil 2: *I can see three sheep and one horse.*
Continue in this way getting other pupils to take part until the description is complete.

2. A game: Who says..?
The children have to guess which animal makes the sound you imitate, for example, ask:

Who says baa-baa?	*The sheep.*
Who says neigh-neigh?	*The horse.*
Who says moo-moo?	*The cow.*
Who says woof-woof?	*The dog.*
Who says miaow-miaow?	*The cat.*
Who says quack-quack?	*The duck.*
Who says cluck-cluck?	*The hen.*
Who says cheep-cheep?	*The chick.*

If you introduce other farm animals other useful sounds are:

hee-haw	*(the donkey)*
gobble-gobble	*(the turkey)*
oink-oink	*(the pig)*
cock-a-doodle-doo	*(the cock).*

You could write the sounds on the board and get the children to copy them near the animals on pages 44 and 45, perhaps in a balloon.

3. Mime the farm animals
Ask a volunteer to mime one of the animals on pages 44 and 45 by imitating the sound or a movement.
Whoever guesses the animal and says the name correctly, then mimes another animal.
Start by practising the vocabulary introduced in this lesson and then gradually extend it to include other typical farm animals (*donkey, turkey, pig, cock*).
If you wish, the game could be extended to include the other animals that the children know in English. This will prove a relaxing and enjoyable break in the lesson and it will prove extremely useful as a way to revise vocabulary.

VII. LET'S SING A SONG

1. "Old Mac Donald" (p. 45)
Explain that this is a traditional English song and that it is about a Scottish farmer called Mac Donald.

2. Close your eyes and listen
Tell the children to close their eyes and to concentrate on the sounds they hear in the song.

3. Look and listen
The pupils follow the text in their books as they listen to the song.

4. Time for play back
The children pretend to sing the song by moving their lips without producing any sounds.

5. Let's sing
At this stage everybody sings the song accompanying it with explanatory movements.
You could suggest additional verses by including other farm animals.

VIII. HOMEWORK

1. Learn the song by heart (p. 45)
The pupils have to learn the song by heart.

2. A poster: What are they doing?
Tell the children that they are going to make a poster which will enable them to practise the use of the present continuous. You could extend the vocabulary relating to actions.
Tell the pupils to cut out pictures of people or animals doing things in the newspaper or magazines.
The students could also bring photos of themselves or members of their families doing particular things.

Unit 7 - Hook's near

Lesson 1 pages 46-47

Materials: a poster, newspaper cuttings or photos brought in by the pupils
Functions: asking who things belong to; expressing position
Structures: *Whose ...?*
Vocabulary: *find, call, hat, footprints, follow, separate, left, right, into, between*

I. WARM-UP

1. Sing the song
Get the children to sing "*Old Mac Donald*".

II. CONSOLIDATION

1. Guess the animal
Tell the students to listen to the descriptions of the animals carefully and to say what the animals are.

They are black and white. You can see them at the zoo. (Zebras).
They are usually pink. They live on the farm. (Pigs).
The can be black and white, or brown. They are big. They live on the farm. (Cows).
They are usually white, but some are black. They live on the farm. (Sheep).
They are grey. They are big. They have got very big ears. You can see them at the zoo. (Elephants).
They are small. They are yellow. You can see them near a hen. (Chicks).

They are brown and orange. They have got very long necks. (Giraffes).

This activity could be performed as a team game. Divide the class into two teams and the first team to guess the animal wins a point. At the end the team with the highest score wins the game.

II. PRESENTATION: Hook's near

1. Look and answer
Tell the children to open their books at pages 46 and 47 and to look at the pictures carefully. Then ask the following questions in L1:
- What does Floppy find?
- What do David and Tommy find?
- What do the children decide to do once they have crossed the bridge? Why?
- Where do the footprints lead? Which group arrives first?
- What do the children find under the pile of leaves?

2. Close your eyes and listen
Get the pupils to close their eyes and to concentrate on what they hear on the cassette. Afterwards they must say which new words or phrases struck them most.

3. Mime the words
The students follow the dialogue in their books and pretend to be the characters in the story by moving their lips when they speak without producing any sounds.

4. Listen and repeat
Check that everybody has understood the dialogue. Then get the children to repeat after each phrase.

III. PRACTICE

1. Right and left
Make sure you have got plenty of space for this activity. Get the children to stand in a semi-circle and tell them to mime some elephants saying:
Now you're elephants. You're big. You're fat. So move like this.
While the children sway on the spot and pretend to be elephants, explain that they must do the movements you say.
Pay particular attention to the directions *right* and *left*.
Then say:
Jump three times (stress that the movements must be slow and clumsy because they are elephants).
Now turn right and walk.
Back to the front.
Turn left and walk.
Back to the front.
Move your head three times.
The pupils will enjoy doing these movements. If necessary, you could do the movements together with the children, otherwise stand in the middle of the semi-circle where you will give the commands and check that they are being carried out correctly.
Then tell the students to mime some frogs (by bending down with their hands on the floor facing slightly inwards).
Then say:
Now you are frogs.
Turn right and jump.
Back to the front.
Turn left and jump.
Back to the front.
The activity can be repeated by suggesting other animals and actions (keep *turn right/left* constant) until all the children do the movements without getting confused.

2. Where's my rubber?
For this activity the desks must be laid out so that the pupils can pass easily from one to the other.
Ask one child to give you an object (a pencil, a rubber etc.) and then to leave the room for a

few seconds. Hand the object to another member of the class who has to hide it.
Call the other child back into the room who asks one classmate:
Where's my (rubber)?
The latter has to give indications so that the other can find the hidden object, for example:
Start here. Go left. Stop. Go right. Stop. Find your (rubber). It's (under the book).

IV. A POSTER: WHAT ARE THEY DOING?

Collect the pictures to be glued onto the poster. In the case of photos, start by asking:
What are you doing here?
If the students do not know the English equivalent of the action being performed, write the infinitive form of the verb on the blackboard.
Glue the photos on the poster and get the pupils to write a simple explanation, for example:
Hello! My name's ... Here I'm (eating an ice cream). It's delicious.
Look at photos of parents or relatives too so as to practise the third person singular personal pronouns. Obviously, the children can write whatever they want beneath the photo (name, age, relationship, physical description etc.).
For the newspaper cuttings, the children could make up details about the people.

V. HOMEWORK

1. Read the dialogue (p. 46-47)
The pupils have to read the dialogue so that they will be prepared to act it out during the following lesson.

Lesson 2 pages 48-49

Materials: a handkerchief or a scarf
Functions: identifying the owner of an object
Structures: *Whose ... is this/that? Whose ... are these/those?*

I. WARM-UP

1. Answer the questions

Ask some questions in L2 about the dialogue in *Unit 7* on pages 46 and 47 to check the pupils' ability to reply using short answers and to give the information requested.

- *Are the children still on the farm?*
- *Is Floppy with them?*
- *What is Floppy carrying in his mouth?*
- *Whose hat is that?*
- *What can the children see on the bridge?*
- *How many children go left and how many go right?*
- *Where do they meet?*
- *What do they find?*

II. CHECKING HOMEWORK

1. Act the dialogue (p. 46-47)

Ask out some pupils to act out the dialogue in front of the class.

III. CONSOLIDATION

1. Guided role-play

Propose a guided role-play along the lines of the dialogue introduced during the

previous lesson. This activity will help the children remember the structures and expressions they have already come across.
Ask four students to take the part of four children of different nationalities. They must follow the indications you give in L1.
You could use the following sequence:

- (Paul) says that London is fantastic.
- (Julie) says that she can not find her cat.
- (Paul) suggests calling him.
- (Julie) calls the cat.
- (John) calls the cat to get it to come to him.
- (Paul) points to the cat.
- (John) points to a hat that the cat has got in its mouth and asks whose it is.
- A child who is following the cat says that it is his hat.
- (Julie) gives the hat back to the child and says sorry.
- The child thanks her and asks whose cat it is.
- (Julie) says that it is her cat.

You will probably have to remind the children of the expressions but gradually the activity will run more smoothly and become more natural.
Later on you could suggest a different role-play with other students.

IV. PRESENTATION AND PRACTICE

1. Whose book is this? It's (name)'s
Walk around the classroom picking up different objects that are on the desks and ask:
Whose (book) is this?
Get the pupils to reply using the genitive:
It's (Mary)'s.
If you consider it necessary, write the short exchange of words on the blackboard as a visual reference for the children.
Continue the activity with the pupils asking the questions.

2. Whose books are these? They're (name)'s
Repeat the previous activity with plural examples.

3. A guessing game
Ask a volunteer to come up to the front of the classroom and blindfold him/her.
The other pupils have to stand in a row.
Turn other pupils around a number of times and lead him/her to a classmate. Guide the volunteer's hand to touch the tip of the other child's nose and ask:
Whose nose is this?
to which the volunteer answers:
It's (name)'s.
You could get him/her to touch the other child's hands and ask:
Whose hands are these?
to which the volunteer answers:
They're (name)'s.
If the volunteer guesses correctly then the other child takes over.
If he/she guesses incorrectly let him/her ask a few questions to make it easier to find out who the other is. For example:
Are you a girl?
Are you tall?
Are you (name)?
If the volunteer is still unable to guess the right name, get another child to continue the game.
Proceed in this way, alternating the parts of the body that are touched (*hair, eyes, hands, arms*, etc.).
The other members of the class participate in the game by saying *right* or *wrong* each time the pupil says the name of a student.

4. Whose are they? (p. 49)
The children have to write the correct phrase in the speech bubbles.
To correct the exercise, one pupil reads out the question and another the answer.
Walk around the classroom checking on spelling.

V. HOMEWORK

1. Find the message (p. 48)
Ask the pupils to find the message on page 48 by writing the first letter of the object in the figure above. The children then write the text in the two speech bubbles at the bottom of the page.

2. Find the opposites (p. 49)
The pupils have to link each word with its opposite.

Lesson 3 pages 50-51

I. CHECKING HOMEWORK

1. Find the message (p. 48)

Ask one member of the class to list the names of the objects in Pat's speech bubble and to write them on the blackboard. The initial letter of each word will give the following phrase: *Whose dog is that?*

With the same procedure correct David's speech bubble which will produce: *It's my dog.*

2. Find the opposites (p. 49)

Play the cassette to check the exercise and to consolidate the pronunciation of the vocabulary.

Tapescript:

Tall/short.
Black/white.
Near/far.
On/under.
Thin/fat.
Here/there.

II. PRACTICE

1. How many opposites do you know?

As a continuation of the previous activity, propose the following "opposites" game. The pupils have to give the opposite of the word you call out.

Write both words on the blackboard (scattered around the board) until the blackboard is full. Afterwards, the students have to copy all the words into their exercise books putting them in two columns. They must put one word in one column and its opposite in the other.

You could use the following terms that the students already know:
this/that
these/those
yes/no
with/without
mum/dad
brother/sister
new/old
happy/sad
up/down
upstairs/downstairs
long/short

2. Jumbled words
Write a phrase from the dialogue in a balloon on the blackboard.
Start with a phrase with only two words such as *Watch out!* but write the words the wrong way round.
The pupils have to put them in the right order.
Continue with sentences containing three, then four, then five words and so on, so that the students gradually acquire the ability to order phrases they already know.
This activity could be done individually, but it would be better to put the students in pairs (mixed ability pairs) to do the exercise together.
For the longer sentences the pairs could compete to see who manages to reconstruct the phrase first. The first ones to finish say: *Stop!*
If the sentence is incorrect, then the game continues to give another pair the possibility to supply to right version.

III. CONSOLIDATION

1. Freer role-play
Ask two volunteers to come up to the front of the class and to follow the indications given in L1 to express themselves in English in a given situation.
They must play the parts of a pupil and a teacher: the teacher comes to class and finds the room in a mess with his/her desk covered in objects.
The teacher asks for an explanation from the pupil.
To make the role-play more realistic tell the children to put different objects on your desk (books, pens, pencils etc.).
Then write *At school* on the blackboard.
The role-play could go as follows:

T: *Teacher*
S: *Student*

T: Enter the classroom and say good morning.
S: Reply.
T: Point out the mess on the desk (*Oh, what a mess!*) and ask who each object belongs to (one at a time).
S: Say who each object belongs to and point at its owner.
T: Ask another pupil what he/she is doing.
S: Answer that the other pupil can't find his/her pencil-case.
T: Find the pencil-case behind a desk and give it to its owner.
S: Thank the teacher.

IV. LET'S SING A SONG

1. "I can't find my hat" (p. 51)
Introduce the song by saying that it is about a very untidy boy.

2. Close your eyes and listen
Tell the children to close their eyes and to concentrate on the words they hear as they listen to the song.
Afterwards the pupils have to say at least two places where the boy must look for his hat.

3. Look, listen and point
The pupils read the words of the song as they listen to the tape and point to the places mentioned.

4. Mime the words
The children pretend to sing the song by moving their lips without producing any sounds.

5. Let's sing
Get everybody to sing the song.

V. HOMEWORK

1. A message from Neverland (p. 50)
The pupils have to read the questions at the bottom of page 50, find the letters and put them in the appropriate space. A phrase will appear vertically.

2. Find ten words (p. 50)
The pupils have to find ten words in the wordsearch.

3. Learn the song by heart (p. 51)
The children must learn the song by heart.

Unit 8 - The mystery's solved!

Lesson 1 pages 52-53

Vocabulary: *mystery, a pair of ..., trousers, gloves, shirt, belt, socks, jacket*

I. WARM-UP

1. Sing the song
Ask the children to sing the song "*I can't find my hat*" all together.
Then, get a few volunteers to sing it once again as if it were a dialogue.

II. CHECKING HOMEWORK

1. A message in Neverland
One pupil reads out the message, which is: *Hook is back.*

2. Find ten words (p. 50)
Ask one member of the class to read the list of words (*wood, tree, bridge, left, right, land, clothes, rock, leaves, footprints*).

III. PRESENTATION: The mystery's solved!

1. Look and answer
Tell the children to open their books at pages 52 and 53 and to look at the illustrations carefully.
Then ask the following questions:
- *Where are the children?*
- *What's behind them?*
- *What does David find?*
- *What is Floppy holding?*
- *What other clothes do they find?*
- *What happens in the last picture?*

2. Close your eyes and listen
Tell the children to close their eyes and to concentrate on what they hear on the cassette.
Afterwards they have to say which new words or phrases struck them most or which phrase they recognised.

3. Mime the words
The pupils follow the dialogue and pretend to be the characters in the book by moving their lips as you play the tape, but without producing any sounds.

4. Listen and repeat
Check that everybody has understood the dialogue, then get the pupils to repeat after each phrase.

IV. PRACTICE

1. Who's wearing what?
Show the class the picture of one article of clothing in the textbook (for example a pair of trousers) and then say:
This is a pair of trousers.
Hands up if you're wearing a pair of trousers.
What colour are your trousers? (asking the individual children).
Continue in this way with all the other articles of clothing and accessories presented. You will probably need to introduce the term *blouse* (for women) besides *shirt* (for men or for unisex sportswear).

2. If you're wearing ...
Once you have practised the vocabulary present the following activity:
If you're wearing socks, say:
"Hello".
If you're wearing blue socks, say:
"Bye-bye".
If you're wearing a pair of jeans, say:
"Please".
If you're wearing a pair of trousers, say:
"Thank you".
At first refer to the pictures in the textbook.
Keep the rhythm quite fast. To make the activity more difficult you could ask the children to repeat a phrase of three or more words.

3. A game: Put on, take off
During this game the children will learn two new verbs and they will be able to practise the vocabulary relating to clothing introduced in this unit.
As you point at an article of clothing or an accessory, say:
Look; a pair of trousers.
Put on the trousers.
The pupils have to mime the action of putting on a pair of trousers.
Continue in the following way:
I've got a pair of shoes here. Put on the shoes, now.
Here is a beautiful belt. Put on the belt and take off the shoes.
Do you like these yellow gloves? Put on the gloves.
Now take off the belt ... and the trousers.
Your feet are cold. Put on these socks.
What are you wearing now?
The students should reply:
The gloves and the socks.
The children probably will not be able to answer because you did not clarify the aim of the game at the beginning. Tell the pupils to concentrate hard and play the game again.
Later on, you could vary the order in which the clothes are put on and taken off, to keep the children stimulated.
If you consider it the case, note down the clothes to be put on and cross them off the list when you say to take them off. In this way you will know exactly which clothes remain on at the end of the activity.

V. HOMEWORK

1. Read the dialogue (p. 52-53)
The pupils have to read the dialogue so that they will be prepared to act it out during the next lesson.

2. My wardrobe
Each child has to draw a picture of an open wardrobe with various articles of clothing in his/her exercise book.
Beside each item they must write its name in English.

Lesson 2 pages 54-55

Materials: flashcards with articles of clothing; a white poster-size sheet of paper
Functions: using possessive adjectives in the third person singular to express possession; expressing an action that is taking place
Structures: *his/her; he/she's wearing ...*
Vocabulary: *skirt, blouse*

I. CHECKING HOMEWORK

1. Act the dialogue (p. 52-53)
Ask a few volunteers to act out the dialogue in front of the class.

2. My wardrobe
The pupils swop exercise books and, with the textbook open at pages 52 and 53, check that the words relating to clothing have been written correctly and put them next to the right article. Walk around the classroom

making sure that the children do not have any problems.

II. CONSOLIDATION

1. Role-play

Propose a guided role-play along the lines of the dialogue presented during the previous lesson. This activity will help the pupils to remember the structures and expressions introduced and make them more aware of their meaning.

Get three pupils to take the part of some English children (or another nationality): they should follow the indications you give in L1:

After an afternoon at the swimming pool, three children have to get dressed:

- (Paul) says that it is late and tells his friends to get dressed quickly.
- (John) looks at the pile of clothes, takes a shirt and asks whose it is.
- (Paul) says that it is Frank's.
- (John) holds up a pair of red trousers and asks whose they are.
- (Paul) says they are Frank's.
- (John) shows his friends a belt and asks if it is Frank's.
- (Frank) says that it isn't his belt, but that it is Paul's.
- (Paul) says that it isn't his.
- (John) laughs and apologises saying that it is his belt.

At first, the pupils will probably need some help in remembering the appropriate structures. Gradually the role-play will proceed more spontaneously. Later on you could get other groups of students to perform the role-play.

2. Clothes

In order to consolidate and to extend the vocabulary relating to clothing, divide the poster-size sheet of paper into two columns. In the left-hand column draw a big snowman and in the right-hand one the sun. Above the snowman, write:

In winter I put on ...

and above the sun:

In summer I put on ...

Write the words relating to typical winter clothing inside the snowman, and the words relating to summer clothing inside the sun. Start with the vocabulary that the children already know and then introduce the words the pupils need to complete the two categories.

Typical winter clothing includes: *trousers, gloves, shirt, blouse, shoes, belt, socks, jacket, hat, dress, anorak, coat, cardigan, pullover, skirt, boots, raincoat, scarf.*

Typical summer clothing includes: *trousers, T-shirt, jeans, belt, shirt, blouse, shoes, jacket, blouse, shorts, skirt, cap, sandals, trainers, dress, swimming costume, swimming trunks, sunglasses.*

For the new vocabulary point it out if a member of the class is wearing one of the articles of clothing or bring some fashion magazines or catalogues to class.

At the end of the activity, the students copy what is on the blackboard into their exercise books.

III. PRESENTATION: his/her

1. His pen or ... her pen?

Ask a boy and a girl to come to the front of the class bringing a few objects with them (a pen, an exercise book, a book).

In turn, each of them shows the other members of the class their objects saying:

This is my (pen).

Then put all the objects together and, pretending not to remember who the objects belong to, ask the other pupils as you point at the boy then the girl:

Is this his (pen) or ... her (pen)?

The rest of the class answer:

It's his/her (pen), pointing at the owner.

Continue like this until the pupils can use the possessive adjectives with ease.

2. Her or his? (p. 54)
Tell the pupils to open their books at page 54. They have to assign the various articles of clothing to Helen or David describing the colour and using the correct possessive adjective.
Play the tape at the end of the activity so that the children can check what they have written.

Tapescript:

Her skirt is red.
Her shoes are blue.
Her socks are blue and white.
Her blouse is white.
Her pullover is red and white.

His shoes are white.
His socks are red.
His pullover is red.
His shirt is yellow.
His trousers are green.

3. Who's Jack? Who's Rosie? (p. 55)
While the children listen to the cassette, they can follow the text in their books to consolidate pronunciation and intonation.
They must identify Jack and Rosie on the basis of the description of their clothes and write their names beneath the right person.

IV. THINK

Ask the pupils to give an example in L1 of the phrases that have been practised, for example:
Mary's got a pen. Her pen is red.
Luke's got a pen. His pen is blue.
Get the students to focus their attention on the possessive adjectives and to deduce the difference in use with respect to their own language.

V. REMEMBER

Write the two possessive adjectives in the third person singular in big letters on the blackboard.
Draw a bow above each word; colour in the bow above *his* blue and the one above *her* pink, so that the difference between the two words can easily be noticed.
Then tell the students to copy the words and the pictures into their exercise books under the heading: *Remember!*

VI. HOMEWORK

1. Describe the other children (p. 55)
Get the pupils to decide on the names they want to give to the other children on page 55. For homework, they have to describe each child's clothing on the basis of the examples provided in the speech bubbles.

Lesson 3 pages 56-57

Materials: flashcards with articles of clothing
Functions: choosing the article of clothing according to the part of the body
Structures: *What can you put on your head/feet/hands?*

I. WARM-UP

1. Answer the questions

Get the children to number the pictures on pages 52 and 53 from one to ten.

Ask the following questions to test the pupils' oral comprehension and their ability to use short answers or to give the information requested without repeating the phrase.

- *Now look at picture number 1:*
  How many children are there?
  How many boys and how many girls are there?
  What is behind the children?
  Are there any frogs in the lake?
  Where's Floppy?
- *Now look at picture number 3:*
  Is Floppy in this picture?
  What is David holding in his hands?
- *What is Floppy carrying in his mouth in picture number 4?*
- *What is David holding in picture number 5?*
- *Is there a pair of trousers in picture number 6?*
  What colour are Hook's shoes?
- *What is Helen holding in her hands in pic-*

ture number 7? Is it brown?
- *Who's wearing Hook's jacket in picture number 9?*
- *Do the children find Hook and Smythe at the end?*

Mime the actions (*hold/carry*) to help the pupils understand the meaning.

II. CHECKING HOMEWORK

1. Describe the other children (p. 55)
Tell the students to take it in turns to read out their description of what one of the characters in the textbook is wearing.
The other pupils can contribute if they wish to.
Walk around the classroom checking on spelling.

III. PRACTICE

1. What are you wearing?
Ask one pupil:
What are you wearing?
The child describes his/her clothing using the vocabulary and structures he/she already knows.
Afterwards, this same person asks another classmate the same question.
The activity continues in this way involving other members of the class.

2. He/She's wearing ...
Present the same structure in the third person singular by writing the following on the blackboard:
He's wearing ....
She's wearing ....
Call a boy and a girl up to your desk and tell the others to take it in turns to say a sentence describing first what the boy is wearing and then what the girl is wearing.
Then tell the pupils to write a description of their deskmate's clothing in their exercise books using the appropriate personal pronoun.
Walk around the classroom checking on what the children are writing.

3. Choose the right clothes
Draw a grid on the blackboard and write the different parts of the body at the top:
Head / Feet / Hands / Legs / Body.
Tell the pupils to copy it into their exercise books.
Use your clothing *flashcards* to introduce the various articles of clothing.
For each flashcard ask:
Where do you wear (socks)?
The class replies giving the part of the body all together:
On our (feet).
Then write the word in the appropriate column, telling the students to do the same in their exercise books.
Proceed like this for all the *flashcards.*

4. What's wrong on Teddy? (p. 56)
Tell the children to open their books at page 56 and to look at Teddy who is dressed rather strangely.
Then ask:
What's wrong on Teddy?
The pupils reply using:
He's wearing ....
giving all the articles of clothing that are in the wrong place.

5. Answer! (p. 56)
Ask the students to look at the speech bubbles at the top of page 56.
Get a volunteer to read the question in the first speech bubble. Then ask another pupil to answer saying:
On my head I can put ...
To answer the questions the pupils can refer to the grid prepared earlier.
Proceed in this way for the other questions.

IV. CONSOLIDATION

1. Role-play

Ask two volunteers to come up to the front of the class and to act out a guided role-play in English.
One of the pupils takes the part of a mother and the other a policeman: the mother has lost her son at the zoo and she describes him to the policeman.
On the blackboard, write:
At the zoo.
Here is a sample role-play:

M: *Mum*
P: *Policeman*

M: Ask with desperation in your voice where your son is and beg the policeman to help you.
P: Ask the lady to describe her son. *(What is he like?)*
M: Say that he has got black hair and brown eyes and that he is short and thin.
P: Ask how old the child is.
M: Reply that he is five.
P: Ask the lady to describe what her son is wearing.
M: Say that he is wearing a pair of jeans, a grey T-shirt and a purple cap.
P: Reply that the child is right there behind her.
M: Express great joy and thank the policeman.
P: Say goodbye politely.

You will probably need to assist the pupils with the suitable expressions at the beginning, but they will gradually gain confidence and competence as the activity proceeds.
Later on the pupils could modify the dialogue as they wish to make the role-play more creative.

V. LET'S SING A SONG

1. "If you're wearing ..." (p. 57)

Introduce the song saying that whoever is wearing a given colour at that moment has to do a particular action.

2. Close your eyes and listen

Tell the children to close their eyes and to concentrate on the words of the song.

3. Look and listen

The pupils listen to the tape as they follow the text in their books.

4. Listen and do

The students who are wearing the colours mentioned in the song have to perform the actions.

5. Mime the words

The children pretend to sing the song by moving their lips without producing any sounds.

6. Let's sing

Everybody sings the song all together and those people who are wearing the colours mentioned have to perform the actions.

VI. HOMEWORK

1. Learn the song by heart (p. 57)

The pupils have to learn the song by heart.

2. Create your own song

Tell the children to make up a new version of the song by inserting an article of clothing in the place of the colours and to make up different actions, for example:
- *If you're wearing a pair of jeans, close your eyes!*
- *If you're wearing a yellow skirt, touch your toes!*

Unit 9 - War is over!

Lesson 1 pages 58-59

Functions: expressing ability and inability
Structures: *I can .../I can't ...*
Vocabulary: *no more, tricks, war*

I. CHECKING HOMEWORK

1. Create your own song
Ask a volunteer to sing his/her version of the song.
While the pupil is singing check the written text and correct the pronunciation if necessary.

II. PRESENTATION: War is over!

1. Look and answer
Tell the children to open their books at pages 58 and 59 and to look at the pictures carefully. Then ask the following questions in L1:
- Why are the children surprised in the first picture?
- What happens to Hook?
- What do you think Hook and Peter are saying?
- Why are the children happy at the end?
- Who appears in the last picture?

Now ask some questions in English?
- *What colour are Pit and Pat's clothes?*
- *Can Hook swim?*
- *How many animals can you see in these comic strips?*
- *How many frogs and how many fish can you see?*

- *Where's the frog in picture number 6?*
Get the pupils to answer either individually or together.

2. Close your eyes and listen
Tell the children to close their eyes and to concentrate on what they hear on the tape. Once they have heard the dialogue the pupils say which new words or phrases struck them most.

3. Mime the words
The students follow the dialogue with their books open and pretend to be the characters in the story by moving their lips without producing any sounds.

4. Listen and repeat
Check that everybody has understood the dialogue especially the expressions *Don't forget me* and *I give up, too.* Then get the students to repeat after each phrase.

III. REVISION

1. I can't ..., but I can ...
Each child has to draw an animal he/she knows on a sheet of paper.
Walk around the classroom asking:
What are you drawing?
Get the children to reply saying:
I'm drawing (a duck).
Then ask other questions about the colour and size of the animal.
Afterwards, draw an animal on the blackboard, for example a fish, with a big balloon within which is written:
I'm a fish.
I can't fly, but I can swim.
Explain that the words underlined are the structures that remain unchanged while the other words (article, noun and verbs) can be varied according to the animal that has been chosen.
After a few oral examples, the students write the phrases inside a balloon on the sheet of paper. Then under the picture they must write a few simple descriptive sentences. For example, referring to the fish, write:
I'm small. I'm red. I live in water.

2. Guess what animal it is
Collect all the pictures and put them on your desk. Call a volunteer up to the front of the class and ask him/her to take one piece of paper, without showing it to the other members of the class. He/she reads out the sentence relating to what the animal can and can't do in the balloon.
Any pupils who think they know the answer intervene saying:
Are you a/an ...?
The volunteer can reply using either:
Yes, I am/No, I'm not or *Right/Wrong.*
The first person to guess the animal, takes the place of the student at the front of the class and continues the game.
If nobody is able to guess, then the pupil reads out one sentence relating to the description of the animal. Continue in this way until all the phrases have been read out.
If the animal still has not been guessed by the end of the description, then the pupil gives the solution and continues the game with another animal.
The game could be played in teams. In this case, divide the class into two groups. A point will be awarded for each animal that is guessed correctly.
The team with the highest score wins the game.

3. Chant the verb "can"
Using the indications provided in the *Welcome Unit II,3,* introduce the following chant to revise and consolidate the affermative, interrogative and negative forms of the verb *can*:
I can, I can, I can, I can.
You can, you can, you can, you can.
He can, he can.

She can, she can.
We can.
You can.
They can.

IV. FAMOUS PEOPLE POSTER

1. What can they do?
Get the children to look at the *Famous People* poster and to insert a phrase which describes what the people are famous for.
The activity could be done in L1 at first, and the English equivalent could be written on the blackboard. You might need to extend the vocabulary to include terms such as:
play tennis
play football
play volleyball
play basketball
Afterwards, point at one of the famous people and provide a model sentence to be put in the speech bubble, for example:
I can sing very well.
Indicate another person and get the students to supply another appropriate phrase.
Then tell the pupils to insert the phrase in the third person singular in the description beneath each person.

V. HOMEWORK

1. Read the dialogue (p. 58-59)
The students have to read the dialogue in preparation for its dramatization during the next lesson.

2. Prepare the "beep" game
Tell the children to underline one word inside each speech bubble while they are reading the dialogue.
Say that the abbreviations count as single words.
Explain to the children that this exercise is in preparation for a game to be played during the next lesson.

3. Bring clothes into the classroom
Tell the pupils to bring an article of clothing (a hat, a belt, a shawl etc.) to school for a fashion show.

Lesson 2 pages 60-61

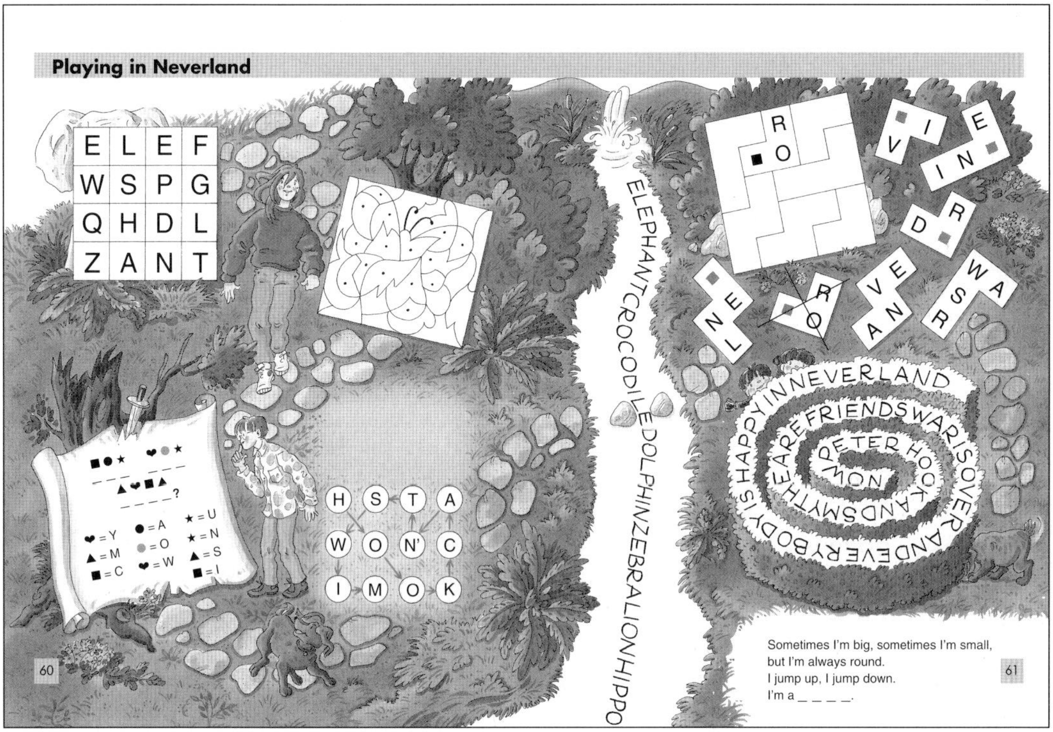

Materials: a handkerchief or a scarf; the articles of clothing brought in by the pupils
Vocabulary: everybody
Phonology: /aun/ as in *down* and *round*; /o:l/ as in *small* and *ball*

I. CHECKING HOMEWORK

1. Act the dialogue (p. 58-59)
Get some students to act out the dialogue in front of the class with their books. Check their intonation and gestures.

2. The "beep" game
Call one child up to the front of the class. He/She has to read out the contents of the speech bubbles inserting a "beep" in the place of the word underlined.
For example:
Here's ... beep... the pirate.
With their books closed the other members of the class have to say together the missing word, like this: *Hook.*

3. Bring the clothes into the classroom
Look through the clothes that the children have brought into class.
Provide any new vocabulary in the following way: write the new words on a piece of paper and attach it to the article of clothing with some sellotape.

II. REVISION

1. A fashion show
Tell the pupils that they are going to hold a fashion show to revise the vocabulary relating to clothing.
Divide the children into two groups. Each group selects a number of models while the other members of the group have to describe the clothes that their classmates are wearing.
Tell them to prepare short descriptive texts in this way:
Model number 1: (the pupils could make up names for the models)
(child's name) is from (country).
He/She's wearing (a funny pair of shoes).
They're (colour), etc.
Her (blouse) is (colour).
Walk around the classroom checking the students' descriptions.
Besides the clothes that have been brought to school, suggest the models wear blouses, T-shirts or jackets the wrong way round and make their clothing as creative as possible.
Once everything is ready, the models in each group pretend to walk along an imaginary catwalk.
Obviously, the children have act out their roles as realistically as possible. You could also photograph the fashion show and then put the photos on the classroom walls with the respective descriptions.

III. PLAYING IN NEVERLAND

At the end of the lesson get the children to play the games on pages 60 and 61 as a moment of relaxation.

- Find the name of the hidden animal (p. 60)
Tell the children to do the first game in the top left-hand corner of page 60 where part of an elephant can be seen behind a grid of letters.
Ask the pupils:
What animal is this?
Once they have answered the question, the children must find the word in the grid.
If you have already introduced the alphabet, you could ask the students to spell the word.

Other possible activities:

a) You could get the pupils to think of one or more words starting with the letters that have not been used. If necessary they could use an illustrated dictionary.
Write the words the students suggest on the blackboard.

b) Using the letters in the grid, the pupils have to find as many words as they can. They can only use the letters in the wordsearch.
The following is a list of words that can be formed:
hand, leg, well, left, pen, all, pen, fat, tall, land, sea, hen, want, snap, tap.
As well as: *feel, spell, sell, wall, shape, sand, shell.*
In order to help the students, you could say a phrase describing the word that has to be found or a phrase containing the word. In the latter case replace the word with a "beep", for example:
You can write and draw with your ... beep ...
Now find the word in the grid. (Hands).

- A secret message (p. 60)
Get the pupils to decode the secret message on the scroll (*Can you swim?*).
Then each child has to reply using *Yes, I can* or *No, I can't but I can ...*

- Follow the arrows (p. 60)
Ask the children to find out what is written in the square with the circles by following the arrows.
Allow a few moments, then ask a volunteer to read out the solution *(Hook can't swim)*.

At this stage, ask:
Is it true or false?
and get the children to reply.

- A guessing game (p. 61)
Read out the clue at the bottom of page 61. Then get one pupil to reread it while the rest of the class mime the words big, small, round, jump up, jump down.
Then say:
Pay attention to the sound: round/down, small/...
The pupils should guess the solution easily: *ball.*

In the case of difficulty, read out the clue once again and while doing so emphasize the various parts such as the rhyme and the movements.
Once the students have found the solution write the words *small/ball* and *round/down* on the blackboard in two columns with the words one beneath the other.
Then ask the pupils to supply other words that rhyme with the ones on the board:
call, tall, all, ...
town, clown, sound, ...
Point out that, particularly in the second case, the words are written differently even though they are pronounced in the same way.

- Colour the dotted spaces (p. 60)
The students have to colour in the dotted spaces to discover the hidden animal. They must then write the name of the animal (*butterfly*) beneath the picture.

- The river (p. 61)
The pupils have to circle the words they recognize in the river and identify the category they belong to.
The words are:
elephant, crocodile, dolphin, zebra, lion, hippo.
The category: *(wild) animals.*

- Solve the puzzle (p. 61)
Tell the children that, by putting the pieces of the puzzle in the right places, they will be able to read a sentence.
(*War is over in Neverland*).

- In the maze (p. 61)
Tell the children to follow the path in the maze to discover the hidden sentences. Get them to write the sentences in their exercise books and to put in the right punctuation. Ask a pupil to read out the sentences in the maze:
Now Peter and Hook are friends. War is over and everybody is happy in Neverland.
Instead of a full stop, a colon could also be used between *friends* and *war.*
Spend a few moments reflecting on the meaning of the sentences in the maze, paying particular attention to the new word *everybody.*

IV. HOMEWORK

1. Playing in Neverland
Tell the children to do the games that were not finished in class for homework.

Lesson 3 pages 62-63

Materials: one poster-size sheet of strong white paper divided into postcard-size worksheets; three or four sets of strips of paper each containing a verse of the song "*I can snap my fingers*"
Vocabulary: *skate, ride a bicycle, move, shake, wink*

I. LET'S PREPARE WORKSHEETS FOR THE CLASS

The games on pages 60 and 61 (together with the ones on pages 7, 48, 50 and 68) could provide an occasion to motivate the pupils to create worksheets to be used in class.

With a wide variety of games to choose from, each pupil will be asked to make up one or more worksheets, using vocabulary and structures presented up until now. It will be a useful and enjoyable way to revise and consolidate.

Amongst all the games, the only complicated one is the puzzle. If anyone wants to have a go at making up one, he/she could do it at home.

For each game, the solution must be provided on another worksheet, both with the same reference number.

Check the games and solutions once they are ready. Put the worksheets with the games in a box and the ones with the solutions in another.

Once the material has been prepared, hand out the worksheets. Ask the pupils to write the solutions in their exercise books as they are doing the games so that the same worksheets can be reused by these students or by others in another class.

II. CONSOLIDATION

1. Role-play

Ask two volunteers to come up to the front of the class to act out a guided role-play. One of them takes the part of a child who can not swim. The child is knocked down by a big wave and has to be saved by a lifeguard.
On the blackboard, write:
At the seaside.
The indications for the role-play could be as follows:

C: *Child*
L: *Lifeguard*

C: Cry out for help and beg someone to come quickly.
L: Say that you are coming.
C: Say that you can't swim.
L: Tell the child to keep calm and not to worry. Once you are safely back on the beach, introduce yourself and ask the child his/her name.
C: Reply.
L: Ask how old the child is;
C: Say that you are ten.
L: Ask if the child is English.
C: Say that you aren't English: say that you are American and live in New York.
L: Offer the child a hamburger.
C: Accept because you are very hungry.
L: Give the child the hamburger.
C: Thank the lifeguard. Say that you feel better now and are no longer afraid. Say goodbye to your new friend.
L: Say goodbye.

During the first performance of the role-play you will probably have to help the pupils with the suitable expressions.
Subsequently, the children could modify various parts of the dialogue (name, nationality, home-town, food that is offered) to make the role-play more creative.

III. PRACTICE

1. Who says what? (p. 62)

Get one child to read out all the phrases in the speech bubbles at the bottom of page 62. Then allow a few moments during which the students match each speech bubble to the right person, by drawing a line with a pencil. To correct the activity, tell one pupil to ask his/her deskmate:
Who says: "I can do magic"?
The other child replies:
Peter says: "I can do magic"
Continue in this way for the other characters in the book.

2. Describe the picture in your own words (p. 62)

Ask a few students to describe the picture on page 62 in their own words, using the structures they already know. The pupils must observe the clothes, the facial expressions and the actions that are being performed.
For example:
Peter is wearing brown shoes, dark green trousers, a light green jacket and a brown belt. He's happy. He can do magic. (Or: *He's doing magic).*

IV. LET'S SING A SONG

1. "I can snap my fingers" (p. 63)

Explain that this song describes various abilities. Play the tape and let the children dance freely to let off energy.

2. Reconstruct the text

Divide the class into groups of eight and

give each group a set of strips each containing a verse of the song. Each pupil will receive a strip. Tell the students to read their strips and see whether they can reconstruct the text on their desks while they listen to the song.
Mime the verbs *shake* and *wink* to help the children with the meaning.
Alternatively, the pupils could reconstruct the text by standing in a line on one side of the class.
The children might need to hear the song more than once to be able to put the strips in the right order.

3. Listen and do
The children listen to the song and mime the actions.

4. Mime the words
The pupils pretend to sing the song by moving their lips without producing any sounds.

5. Let's sing and dance
Everybody sings and mimes the actions all together.

V. HOMEWORK

1. Learn the song by heart (p. 63)
The children have to learn the song by heart.

2. Describe the picture in your own words (p. 62)
Tell the pupils to write the description of the picture on page 62 in their exercise books.

Unit 10 - Another trick!

Lesson 1 pages 64-65

Functions: offering something; expressing a preference
Structures: *Would you like a/an/some ...? I prefer ...*
Vocabulary: *cheers! dinner, chicken, a piece of, carrots, crazy, plates, empty, bowl*

I. WARM-UP

1. Sing the song
Tell the children to sing together "*I can snap my fingers*" accompanying by the appropriate actions.

2. What are they doing? (p. 63)
Open your book at page 63 and hold it up so that everybody can see it. Point at the characters and say:
What is he/she doing?
The pupils reply using the continuous form of the verb.

3. Copy in the right column
Tell the children to update their list of verbs (ref: U6.L1.II,2) by adding the ones in the song.

II. CHECKING HOMEWORK

1. Describe the picture in your own words (p. 62)
Walk around the classroom to correct the descriptions individually.

III. PRESENTATION: Another trick!

1. Look and answer
Get the children to open their books at pages 64 and 65 and to look at the illustrations of the comic-strip carefully. Then ask the following questions in L1:
- What are all the characters in the story doing?
- What food do you recognize on the table?
- What does Peter like doing?
- What happens at the end?

2. Read silently and underline the words you know
Before playing the tape, tell the children to read the text silently and to underline the words they know. The abbreviations are considered one word and *Hmmm, Hey, Ha, ha, ha!* all count.

3. Close your eyes and listen
Tell the children to close their eyes and to concentrate on what they hear on the cassette.

4. Mime the words
The pupils follow the text in their books and pretend to be the characters who are speaking on the tape by moving their lips.

5. Listen and repeat
Check that everybody has understood the dialogue, then get the pupils to repeat after each phrase.

IV. PRACTICE

1. A guessing game: Full or empty?
Take a pencil sharpener and, holding it in one hand, say *full*.
Then show the class the other hand, with no pencil sharpener and say *empty*. Repeat a few times, alternating one hand with the other.
Put both hands behind your back and then stretch out your closed fists in front of one child and ask: *Full or empty?*
The pupil has to indicate which hand he/she thinks the pencil sharpener is in saying: *Full.*
If he/she guesses correctly then he/she asks another pupil the same question, otherwise he/she has to pay a small penalty (eg. repeat a sentence a number of times, carry out some orders, etc.).

2. Would you like ...?
Go up to one student with a flashcard of some food (for example, an apple) and offer it to the child saying:
Would you like an apple?
Get the pupil to accept (*Yes, please*) or refuse (*No, thank you*).
Continue in this way providing examples with *a/an/some*.

3. Offering food
Hand out the *flashcards*, so that each child has one.
If you do not have enough *flashcards*, draw a picture of some fruit or another type of food on a sheet of paper.
Each pupil will ask another member of the class: *Would you like a/an/some ...?* followed by the food on the flashcard.
Once a student has answered, he/she offers his/her deskmate something and so on round the class until the pupil who asked the first question is reached.
The children keep the *flashcards* for the following activity.

4. What do you prefer? Carrots or potatoes?
To practise the verb *to prefer* ask the children about their preferences, giving them two alternatives, for example:
Which do you prefer? Carrots or potatoes?
Each pupil answers:
I prefer (carrots).

5. Expressing preference
Using the flashcards, go up to one pupil and offer him/her something:
Would you like (an ice cream)?
The child can reply either affermatively, or negatively expressing a preference:
No, thanks. I don't like ice cream. I prefer (coke).
Proceed in this way until everybody has had a chance to ask and answer a question.

V. REMEMBER

Write the short dialogues on the blackboard and get the students to copy them into their exercise books under the heading: *Remember!*

VI. HOMEWORK

1. Read the dialogue (p. 64-65)
The pupils have to read the dialogue in preparation for its dramatization in class;

2. Let's prepare for the "beep" game.
As they read the dialogue the pupils have to underline one word in each speech bubble.

Lesson 2

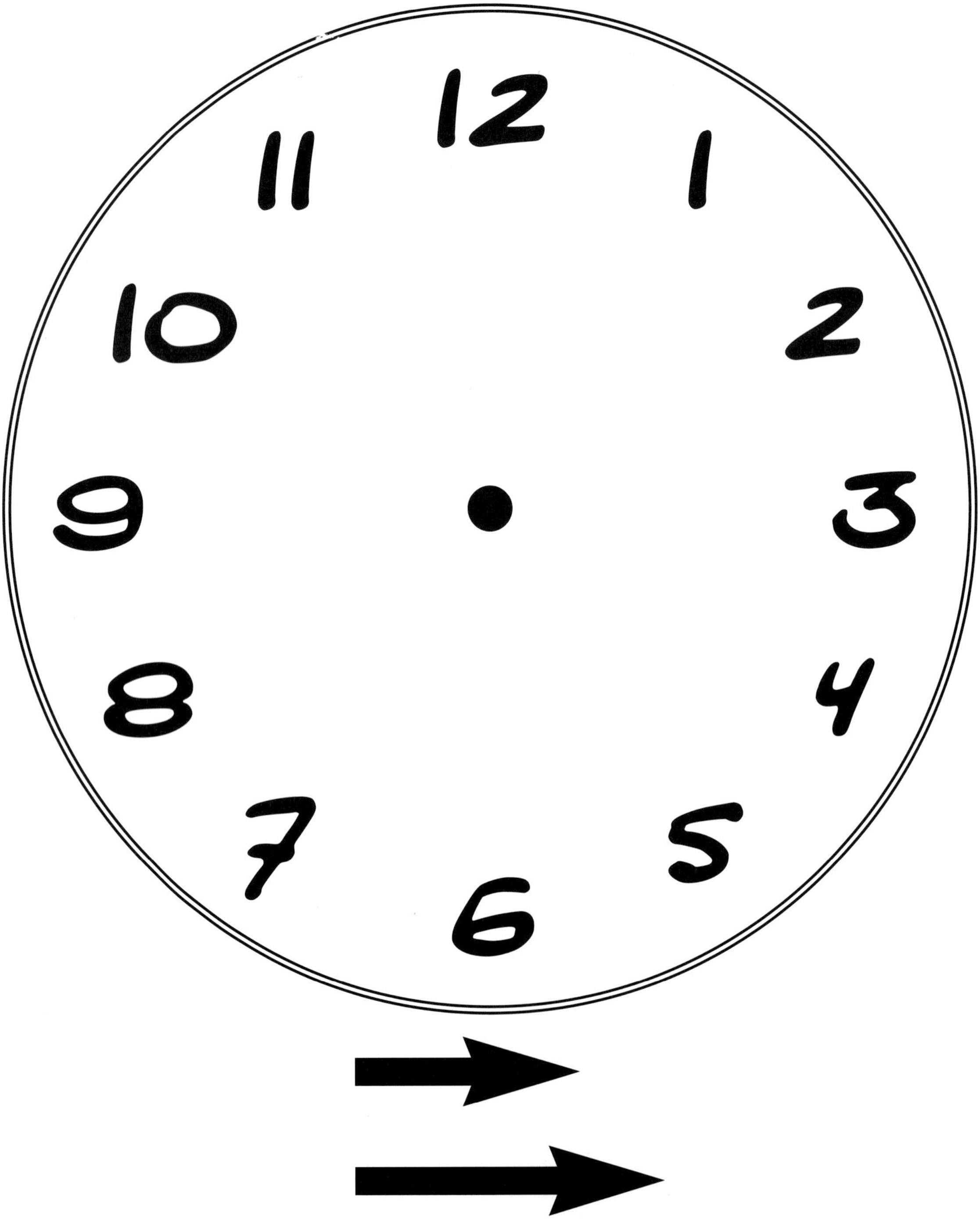

Lesson 2 pages 66-67

Look and answer

What are the boys doing? ....

Is there a cake on the table? ....

Is Helen drinking? ....

What's Peter doing? ....

Is Smythe eating? ....

Is Floppy drinking? ....

What's Hook doing? ....

What's Floppy doing? ....

Are there any apples on the table? ....

Is Helen sitting at the table? ....

66

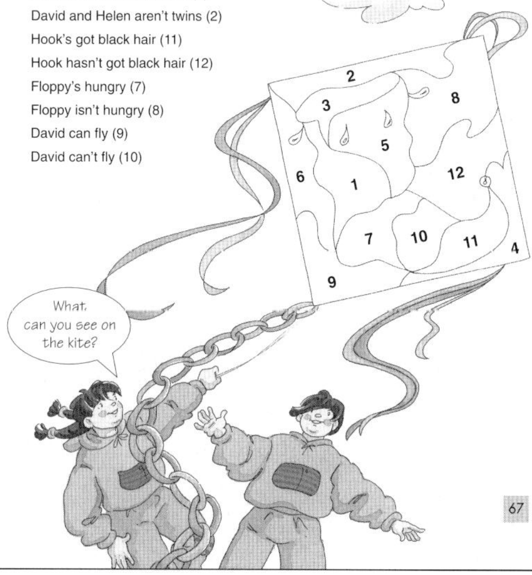

Colour the right answer

Peter can do magic (3)
Peter can't do magic (4)
Now Hook and Peter are friends (5)
Now Hook and Peter aren't friends (6)
David and Helen are twins (1)
David and Helen aren't twins (2)
Hook's got black hair (11)
Hook hasn't got black hair (12)
Floppy's hungry (7)
Floppy isn't hungry (8)
David can fly (9)
David can't fly (10)

67

Materials: the picture of the clock glued onto some cardboard
Functions: *telling the time (on the hour, quarter to and past, half past)*
Vocabulary: *a quarter to, a quarter past, half past, kite*

I. WARM-UP

1. Full or empty?
Get the students to play the full or empty game again, but introduce a counting song to find the hidden object.
The pupil who has to guess taps the closed fists and says:
One, two
dee-dee, dee-doo,
this is empty,
this is full.

II. CHECKING HOMEWORK

1. Act the dialogue (p. 64-65)
Get a few volunteers to act out the dialogue in front of the class with their books open. Make sure they pay attention to intonation and gestures.

2. The "beep" game
Ask one pupil to come up to the front of the class and read out the dialogue on pages 64 and 65. As the child reads it out he/she has to replace the underlined word with a "beep". The rest of the class say the missing word together.

III. PRESENTATION: Time

1. What time do you have dinner?
Referring to the situation in the textbook, dinner with friends, do a small survey to find out what time the pupils usually have dinner. Ask them:
What time do you have dinner?
The children reply in L1.
Show the. class the clock that you have prepared at home and move the hands so that they are on the hour (for example: *7 o'clock*) and a quarter to the hour (*a quarter to seven*).
Then repeat:
It's (seven) o'clock.
It's a quarter to (seven).
Once you have consolidated the expression *a quarter to*, introduce *a quarter past* by alternating the two. Finally introduce *half past* in the same way.
Draw four clocks on the blackboard with different times: 6.45, 7.00, 7.15, and 7.30. Above each clock write the expressions *a quarter to, o'clock, a quarter past, half past.*
Then, referring to the board, ask the class the initial question:
What time do you have dinner?
The pupils have to express themselves in English this time.
Point out that 13.00 and 14.00 etc. are not used to express the afternoon hours in English, but 1.00, 2.00 etc. You can use *a.m.* (*anti meridiem*) for the morning hours or *p.m.* (*post meridiem*) for the afternoon hours.
At the end of the activity, tell the students to copy what is on the blackboard into their exercise books.

IV. PRACTICE

1. What's the time, Peter Pan?
Write the following sentences on some sheets of paper (one for each sheet):

It's 7.15	*It's time to get up.*
It's 7.30 am	*It's time to have breakfast.*
It's 8.00 am	*It's time to go to school.*
It's 12.30 pm	*It's time to go home.*
It's 1.00 pm	*It's time to have lunch.*
It's 2.30 pm	*It's time to do your homework.*
It's 4.45 pm	*It's time to have a snack.*
It's 5.00 pm	*It's time to play.*
It's 6.00 pm	*It's time to watch your favourite TV programme.*
It's 7.00 pm	*It's time to have dinner.*
It's 8.30 pm	*It's time to wash.*
It's 9.00 pm	*It's time to go to bed.*

Give each pair of students a sheet of paper.
Pointing at the pair that has to answer ask the question:
What's the time, Peter Pan?
One of the two reads out the time and the other the rest of the phrase.

V. REVISION

1. Describe the picture (p. 66)
Use the picture on page 66 to revise vocabulary and structures that the students already know by asking them to describe what they can see, particularly the actions being performed by the various characters.

2. Look and answer (p. 66)
Get the pupils to answer the questions on page 66 individually.
To correct the activity, ask the questions one at a time getting one pupil to answer each one.
The rest of the class have to say whether the reply is the same as theirs.
If not, the others have to read out their answer.
Walk around the classroom checking on spelling.

VI. HOMEWORK

1. Colour the right answer (p. 67)
Tell the pupils to open their books at page 67. Explain that at home they have to colour in the spaces in the square with the numbers which correspond to the phrases that they consider are true. In this way, an object will appear and they will have to answer Pat's question.

2. Draw 10 clocks
The pupils have to draw 10 clocks with numbers, but without any hands.

Lesson 3 pages 68-69

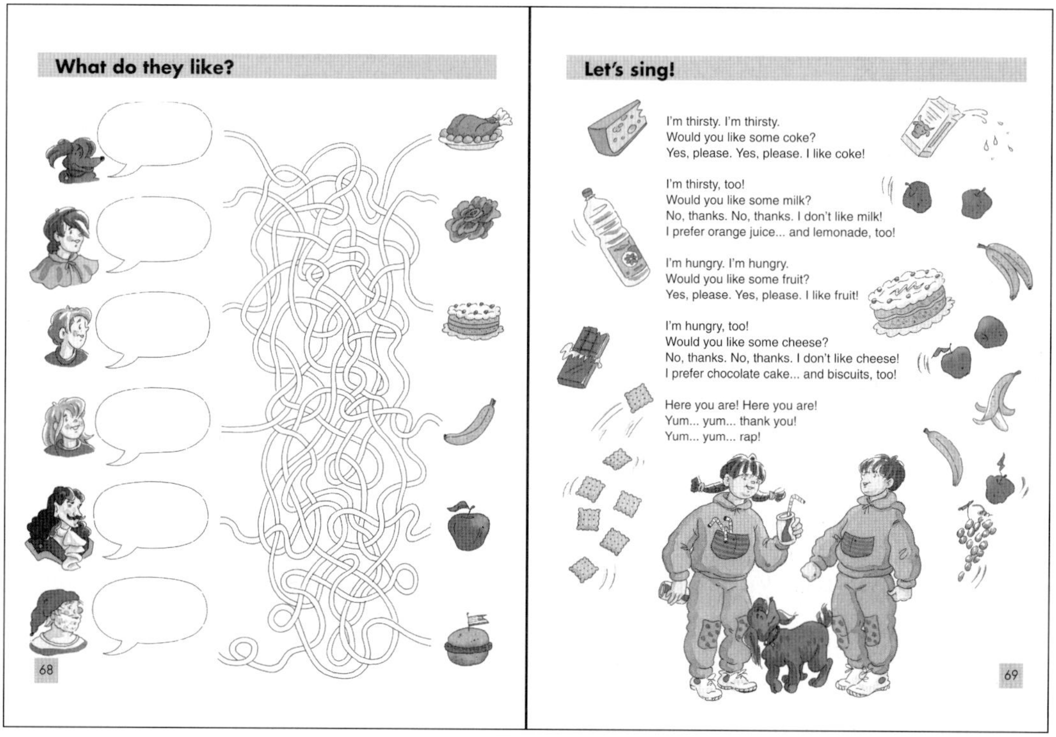

Functions: expressing hunger and thirst, offering something, accepting and refusing
Structures: *I'm hungry, I'm thirsty, Would you like a/an/some ...?, Yes, please / No, thanks*

I. WARM-UP

1. Answer the questions
Once you have presented the new vocabulary relating to the food on the table (*coconuts, water, wine*), ask some questions in English about the illustrations on pages 64 and 65:

- *What food can you see on the table?*
- *Where is David sitting?*
- *Is Smythe wearing shoes?*
- *How many pirates join the group?*
- *Do they all feel happy?*
- *Peter is playing a trick. Which food disappears?*
- *Is Floppy's bowl full or empty?*
- *Which food can you see in the last picture?*

Get the children to reply either individually or all together.

II. CHECKING HOMEWORK

1. Colour the right answer (p. 67)

Ask one child to answer Pat's question (*I can see a shoe*).

III. CONSOLIDATION

1. Role-play

The following role-play is one way to check whether the structures presented in the dialogue have been assimilated.

The children have to imagine that two friends are having dinner.

George has just come back from a trip abroad and his friend, Luke has invited him to dinner.

- Luke's mother says that dinner is ready.
- Luke raises his glass to George and says hurray.
- Luke's family all join in by raising their glasses.
- Luke's mother offers George something to eat and asks if he wants some chicken.
- George says that he would and adds that he likes chicken.
- Luke's mother asks if he prefers water or coca-cola.
- George says that he prefers coca-cola.
- Then the lady offers him some potatoes.
- George refuses saying that he doesn't like potatoes. He adds that he prefers carrots.
- Luke's mother hands them to him.
- George thanks her.
- When George sees the cake, he looks very surprised and asks if he can have a big piece.
- Luke's mother says that of course he can have a big piece.
- George says that he likes the cake very much and adds that it is delicious.
- Luke's mother thanks him and then asks if he wants some fruit saying that there are some apples, pears, bananas and kiwis.
- George refuses politely with an expression on his face showing that he has really eaten too much!

2. What do they like? (p. 68)

The pupils have to fill in the speech bubbles using the structure *I like* followed by the food found on the other side of the page.

When you correct the exercise make sure that the pupils have been able to discriminate between the *countable* (*bananas, apples, hamburgers*) and *uncountable* nouns (*chicken, salad, cake*).

IV. PRACTICE

1. Write the time you hear

Tell the students to open their exercise books at the page with the ten clocks.

Once you have revised the expressions *a quarter to, a quarter past* and *half past* (using your paper clock) explain that the children have to draw the hands on the clocks according to the time they hear.

For example:

It's three o'clock.
It's a quarter past ten.
It's half past two.
It's a quarter to five.
It's seven o'clock.
It's half past nine.
It's a quarter to eight.
It's half past six.

It's a quarter to eleven.
It's midday.
To correct the activity, show the time on your paper clock.

2. Living clock
You need plenty of space for this activity.
Tell 12 pupils to each write one number (from 1 to 12) on a piece of paper and to stand in a circle showing the numbers. They represent the hours on the face of a living clock.
Get another 2 children to stand in the middle. One of them stretches out his/her arms: this is the minute hand.
The other stretches out only one arm: it is the hour hand.
According to your indications, the other pupils have to take it in turns to enter the circle and position the hands of the clock correctly.

Extention:
You could suggest one of the phrases practised during the previous lesson for example:
It's time to have breakfast.
What time is it?
A pupil has to go into the circle, position the hands of the clock and say the right time:
It's (eight) o'clock/half past eight/etc.

V. LET'S SING A SONG

1. "I'm thirsty" (p. 69)
Get the pupils to listen to the song and to dance all together.

2. Listen and say
Ask the children whether they have understood what the song is about. Then play the cassette again.
Afterwards, ask the students to name the food that is mentioned. Write the suggestions on the blackboard.
Let the children listen to the song once again.

3. Time for playback
With their books open the children pretend to sing the song by moving their lips but without producing any sounds.

4. Let's sing
The pupils sing the song all together.

Revision

After the tenth lesson, it is advisable to consolidate the new structures that have been introduced, particularly in the last five units, so that all the pupils can reach the same level.
With this in mind, both the second revision game on pages 70 and 71 and the other activities presented here provide interesting and relaxing ways to revise vocabulary and grammatical structures for a few lessons before you test your pupils.

SNAKES AND LADDERS

Materials: one dice; one marker for each student.
Purpose: comprehension of the instructions of the game; revision of vocabulary and structures that have already been presented.

This game is played with a dice in pairs.
Beginning at *Start*, each child tries to beat his/her partner to the *Finish*.
Explain that everybody needs a marker (a rubber, a pencil sharpener etc.) which will be moved along the squares according to the number obtained when the dice is thrown.
Before starting the game, explain that the winner has to obtain the exact number to land on *Finish*. If the number on the dice is more then he/she has to count backwards along the squares.
Introduce a few expressions in L2 that will be useful during the game:
Throw the dice.
What number is it?
Move your counter.
It's my/your turn.
Miss a turn.
A ladder. Go up the ladder.
A snake. Go down the snake.
I'm the winner!
Stress that the children have to use L2 throughout the game and tell them that they will miss a turn each time they speak in L1.
If the pupils land on squares 1, 6, 29 and 37 they must carry out some simple tasks which are described on page 70.
Walk around the classroom while the children play the game checking that the rules are being obeyed and correcting any pronunciation mistakes.

TEN MORE REVISION ACTIVITIES

1. WHAT'S HAPPENING?

Purpose: to consolidate the continuous form.

Divide the class into four groups: *elephants, crocodiles, lions and hippos.* Explain that each group has to do the actions suggested.
With surprise in your voice start the game saying:
What's happening?
The elephants are flying!
The crocodiles are singing!
The lions are jumping!
The hippos are dancing!
Gradually increase the speed of what you are saying as you address the groups.
For the time being propose the same actions.
Afterwards, vary the actions, saying for example:
The elephants are singing!
The hippos are jumping!
The lions are flying!
The crocodiles are dancing!
Other actions could include: *eating, drinking, sleeping, swimming, climbing trees, turning around, stamping their feet, shaking their head, going right, going left, walking around, calling Floppy, looking up/down, repeating:*
"I am happy".
You will create a playful atmosphere and the children's need to move will be satisfied.

2. INFORMATION GAP ACTIVITY

Materials: sheets of paper with a six-square grid.
Purpose: to consolidate the structures *Are there any ...? I've got some ...*

The pupils do this activity in pairs sitting opposite one another.
Each child has to draw a grid with six squares (numbered from 1 to 6 in the same order) on a sheet of paper or in his/her exercise book. Each square represents a *field.*
Without letting his/her partner see, one child from each pair, (A), writes the number and name of the animals grazing in each field, for example:

1 6 COWS	**2** 3 SHEEP	**3** 5 HENS
4 8 DUCKS	**5** 2 HORSES	**6** 10 PIGS

The other pupil (B) has to ask questions in order to fill in his grid in the same way.
Examples of structures to use could be:
B: Are there any cows?/ Have you got any cows?
A: Yes, there are/ Yes, I have.
B. Are they in field number 3?
A: No./No, they aren't.
B: Are they in field number 1?
A: Yes./Yes, they are.
B: How many are there?
A: There are 6.
At the end the pupils compare grids.
Afterwards, the roles could be reversed and the grid redone.

3. WHOSE BAG IS THIS?

Purpose: to consolidate the genitive.

Tell the children to copy the following situations from the blackboard with the respective questions, or if you wish, prepare a photocopy for each child.
In pairs, the pupils have to answer the questions relating to the pictures on pages 34 and 35. They must identify the owner of the shopping bag on the basis of the description of its contents.
The description of the various bags and the respective questions could be as follows:
1. *In this shopping bag there's a pair of jeans. Whose bag is this?*
2. *In this shopping bag there's a lead. Whose bag is this?*
3. *In this shopping bag there's a bottle of orange juice. Whose bag is this?*
4. *In this shopping bag there's a cassette. Whose bag is this?*
5. *In this shopping bag there's a book. Whose bag is this?*
6. *In this shopping bag there's a pair of shoes. Whose bag is this?*

You could answer the first question as an example:
It's Helen's (bag).
The pupils work in pairs giving a written answer. Afterwards, correct the activity orally getting different students to read out their answers.

4. FIND SOMEONE WHO'S WEARING

Materials: a handkerchief to use as a blindfold
Purpose: to consolidate vocabulary relating to clothing and the continuous form.

Get the children to stand in a circle. Call one pupil into the middle, blindfold him/her and turn the child around a few times.
Start the game by saying:
Now find someone who's wearing (blue shoes).
Establish beforehand how many guesses are allowed.

The child that is blindfolded has to go and touch a classmate and ask:
Are you wearing (blue shoes)?
The other person replies using:
Yes, I am/No, I'm not.
If the child guesses correctly within the established number of goes, then the pupil that has been touched goes to the middle of the circle and continues the game.
If, to the contrary, the blindfolded child is unable to guess, he/she has to do a small forfeit and another student is chosen to continue the game.

5. WRITE ON YOUR FRIEND'S BACK

Purpose: to revise vocabulary relating to parts of the body, animals, clothing, food etc.

Divide the class into two teams and call one pupil from each team out to the front of the class.
The teams take it in turns to play. For simplicity we'll call the two teams A and B, but the pupils could choose names as they wish (*the lions/the tigers...*).
A child from team B stands behind one of his/her classmates from the opposite team.
Making sure that the pupil from team A is unable to see, write a word (a noun in L2) proposed by pupil B on the blackboard.
Pupil B then writes the same word very slowly on A's back with pauses between the letters.
If A guesses the word immediately he/she wins two points, otherwise before trying to guess a second time, pupil A must ask his/her team three questions to simplify the identifcation of the word.
For example:
Where can I see it?
Is it an animal/a food/an object?
Can I eat/drink/wear/use it?
Is it (size/colour)?

If the child is unable to understand the word, then his/her team wins no points.
The team with the highest score, once each member has had a go, wins the game.

6. SCRABBLE

Purpose: to revise the spelling of words.

Write a word in the middle of the blackboard. The pupils, divided into two teams, stand in two lines on either side of the board.
In turns, a member of each team writes a word that crosses the other word, like a crossword, using a letter that is already on the blackboard.

```
    H
    A
    TROUSERS
      R
      A
ELEPHANT
      G
  HOUSE
```

Decide whether the other members of the team can help in case of difficulty. Fix a time limit within which, if a word has not been inserted, the opposite team has a go.
The team that supplies the most words wins the game.
You could make the game more difficult by establishing the minimum number of letters that the word must contain, or by allowing each team to cross up to three words. In the latter case, the team that has managed to cross the most number of words wins the game.

7. DRAMA

Purpose: to consolidate the grammatical structures presented in units 6, 7, 8, 9 and 10.

Tell the children to act out the adventures of the characters in *Magic!*
Choose different children for each unit. Those pupils who do not act out the dialogues could choose some songs to sing either individually or in groups.
This activity gives you the opportunity to do a different type of lesson during which the "actors" or "singers" have the audience, that is their classmates, in front of them.
You could also get the children to dress up to make the performance all the more theatrical.

8. RECONSTRUCT THE DIALOGUE

Materials: a set of pieces of paper (obtained by dividing an A4 sheet into four parts).
Purpose: to recognize structures and reconstruct a dialogue.

Divide the class into groups of three or four and give each group a set of pieces of paper.
Tell each group which dialogue (from which unit) they have to work on.
The pupils have to draw a speech bubble on each piece of paper, copy down the contents and write the name of the character to whom it refers at the top.
Once all the material has been prepared, shuffle the pieces of paper and fix a time limit within which the dialogue has to be reconstructed.
You could assign a different dialogue to each group and then get them to swop with another group.
At the end of the activity, put each set in an envelope.

9. MAKE AS MANY SENTENCES AS YOU CAN FIND

Purpose: to make affermative, interrogative and negative sentences.

Scatter the following words on the blackboard:
I, you, they
like, prefer
would, do, don't
hamburgers, apples, milk, chocolate, kiwis, etc.
Before starting the activity, ask the students what type of sentences they can make (relating to preference, likes and dislikes, offers, requests).
Get the pupils to work in groups of three. Within a fixed time limit they have to make up as many sentences as possible.
The group that forms the most correct sentences wins the game.

10. OPPOSITE SNATCH

Materials: an object to place on a desk that can be easily grabbed (a skittle, a pencil case); a list of the opposites you want to practise; small pieces of paper to write on.
Purpose: to consolidate opposites.

You need plenty of space for this activity.
Divide the class into two groups and get the members of each group to stand in a line some distance from the other group.
Give each member of team A a piece of paper with a sentence and each member of team B a piece of paper with the respective opposites.
In the middle, between the two lines, place an object on a desk or a chair.
The first pupil from one of the teams reads out his/her sentence and someone from the other team reads out the opposite sentence.
When they have finished speaking, both pupils have to run to the middle to grab the object.
The person who manages to grab the object first wins a point for his/her team.
Replace the object and the game continues until everybody has had at least one go. The

team with the highest score wins the game. Make sure that the pupils start running only when the second student has finished reading his/her sentence, also because the sentence read out by the second pupil might be incorrect.
The following list of sentences can be used for this game in addition to simple adjectives, adverbs etc.

Go up - Go down.
This is black - This is white.
I'm tall - I'm short.
My cat is fat - Your cat is thin.
I've got a long pencil - I've got a short pencil.
The pirates are here - The pirates are there.
Her skirt is blue - Her skirt is red.
On the desk there's a book - Under the desk there's a book.

TEST 2

NAME .... MARK ....

1. Listen and tick the correct picture

Set 1

Set 2

Set 3

Set 4

2. Read and draw

a. Peter's belt is in the cupboard.
b. David's pullover is on the sofa.
c. Helen's shoes are near the wardrobe.
d. Floppy's lead is under the table.
e. Pat's T-shirt is in the wardrobe.
f. Toby's socks are on the chair.

a.	**b.**	**c.**
d.	**e.**	**f.**

3. Add to the sequence

a. finger, toe, head, ...
b. yellow, brown, black, ...
c. two, four, six, ...
d. zebras, dolphins, tigers, ...
e. sheep, horse, dog, ...
f. swim, fly, move, ...

4. Complete the bubbles

Choose from these verbs:

fly, jump, climb, swim, dance, drink, sing, stamp, touch, move.

What are they doing?

Pit and Pat ....
....

Peter ....
....

Helen ....
....

Hook and Smythe ....
....

TEST 2 - NOTES FOR THE TEACHER

The **first exercise** in *Test 2* tests listening skills.
Explain that you are going to read out a short text and the pupils have to tick the correct picture.
Read out the texts at normal speed the first time leaving a brief pause between one description and the next.
Afterwards, read out all the descriptions without any pauses to enable the pupils to check their choices.

Set 1: *Would you like some fruit? Look on the table. There are some apples in the bowl.*

Set 2: *What can Rudy do? He can't sing and he can't play tennis... but he can swim very well.*

Set 3: *What do you prefer, tea or milk? Well, I don't like milk and I don't like tea very much. I can see some orange juice over there. Can I have some, please?*

Set 4: *Where's Susan? I don't know but... wait a moment. Yes, I can see her. She's in the garden. She's reading a book under the tree.*

The **second exercise** is a reading activity. The pupils have to read the text and draw the description.
In the **third exercise** the children have to add a word that belongs to the same category.
In the **fourth exercise** the pupils have to complete the speech bubbles with the appropriate form of the present continuous choosing from the verbs listed.

CORRECTION OF TEST No 2

Correct the test in class during the following lesson and involve all the children as it will be a moment for revision. Distribute the test sheets making sure that each pupil receives another person's test.
This should stimulate the pupils to pay attention while you help them correct a test that is not theirs.
With regard to the **first exercise** read out the description relating to each set of pictures then ask one student which picture he/she has ticked. Check that the child has chosen the right figure and ensure that the other members of the class have done so too. Proceed in this way for the other three sets of illustrations.
Move on to the **second exercise**. Ask one child to read out the sentence and to say in L1 where he/she has placed the article of clothing or the accessory. Point out that in the case of shoes and socks it is necessary to draw at least two. The pupils have to point out any errors.
For the **third exercise** you could proceed in the following way:

Teacher:	*Look at (a.): finger, toe, head. What are they? Animals, colours, parts of the body?*
Pupils:	*Parts of the body.*
Teacher:	*Yes, right. Now tell me the name of another part of the body.*
Pupils:	*Leg, nose, ...*

Write the words on the blackboard so that the children can check the spelling.
In the case of mistakes, tell the children to underline the wrong word and to add the correct one next to it or above it so that the classmate can see the error and understand his/her mistake.
For the **fourth exercise** get the pupils to take it in turns to read out the sentences in the

speech bubbles. Write what they say on the blackboard.
Once you have finished correcting the test, put your marking criteria on the blackboard.
The children count the mistakes on the test sheet they are correcting, write down the mark and then hand them back to you.
Check them briefly, write the marks in your register, then give each test sheet back to the person who did the test.
At this stage, each child can see the mistakes he/she has made.
Tell them to write any wrong words a number of times in their exercise books to ensure they remember the correct spelling.
The children take their test sheets home and get one of their parents to sign it.
The next lesson they hand the tests back to you and you keep them until the end of the academic year.

Unit 11 - Stories around the fire

This unit is presented differently as it is divided into two parts.
The first part presents a lesson based on the dialogue in the textbook and activities to practise the structures found in the dialogue. The pupils will probably already know most of the structures.
The second part, however, is dedicated to the stories and legends narrated by Peter Pan's friends as they sit around the fire.
After an initial introduction, six distinct sections follow, one for each story. Decide beforehand whether you want to dedicate one lesson to each story, together with the activities, or to do the activities during the course of two or more lessons.

Part 1 - Lesson 1 pages 72-73

Functions: asking what to do; inviting someone to do something; making suggestions
Structures: *What do we do now?; Who wants to ...?/Would you like to ...?; What about ...?*
Vocabulary: *stories, fire, different, start*

I. WARM-UP

1. Would you like to sing a song?
Ask the children if they would like to sing a song chosen from the ones they already know. Say:
Would you like to sing a song?
Which one would you like to sing?

II. PRESENTATION: Stories around the fire

1. Look and answer
Tell the children to open their books at pages 72 and 73 and to look at the illustrations carefully. Then ask the following questions in L1:

- What's left over at the end of the meal?
- Do you think Floppy is satisfied with what he has eaten?
- What do the children do after dinner?
- What do you think they are going to do around the fire? (to play a game, tell jokes, sing ...).

2. Silent reading

Tell the pupils to read the dialogue and to underline all the words they know.
As the children dictate the words write them on the board. If you are unsure of their choice ask them where they have already come across the word. To make the activity more creative, you could ask the students to make up sentences containing one or more of the words on the blackboard.

3. Close your eyes and listen

Get the children to close their eyes and to concentrate on the sounds they hear as they listen to the tape.

4. Mime the words

The students follow the text in their books and pretend to be the characters in the story by moving their lips as they speak without producing any sounds.

5. Listen and repeat

Play the cassette again getting the pupils to repeat after each phrase.

III. PRACTICE

1. Would you like to ...? Who wants to ...?

Ask the children, either individually or as a group, to do particular actions to practise the structures:
Would you like to ...? Who wants to ...?
to which the pupils answer *Yes/No* and *Me.*
You could ask the following questions:
- *Would you like to draw something on the blackboard?*
- *What would you like to draw?*
- *Would you like something to eat/drink?*
- *What would you like?*
- *Who wants to count from 1 to 20?*
- *Who wants to mime a giraffe?*
- *Who wants to read the dialogue?*

If the children already know these two structures, because they form part of the classroom language, you do not need to spend too much time on this activity.

2. Mini dialogues

Tell the class that they are going to do some mini dialogues to practise asking for something or making suggestions.
Since these structures are not new the pupils should not find this activity difficult.
However, if necessary, let the children keep their books open for reference.

First dialogue:
- Peter says that dinner is over.
- David asks what they could do.
- Peter suggests sitting around the fire.
- Helen agrees.

Second dialogue:
- Hook says that he is hungry.
- Smythe offers him some chicken and carrots.
- Hook doesn't want any and suggests fish and chips.
- Smythe says that he doesn't like fish.

Third dialogue:
- David says that the lesson is over.
- Helen asks what they should do now.
- David suggests going to Old Mac Donald's farm.
- Helen doesn't agree and suggests going for a walk in the park.

Fourth dialogue:
- Mary offers Mark a Coca-cola.
- Mark refuses saying that he doesn't like Coca-cola.

- Mary suggests an orange juice.
- Mark refuses once again and says that he prefers lemonade.
- Mary offers him some lemonade.
- Mark thanks her.

3. Suggest what to do

Tell the children to get into pairs. Give each pair a sheet of paper.
Dictate some phrases which the children have to write in red. Tell them to leave one line after each phrase for the suggestions which must be written in blue using the structures:
What about a .../an ... or *Let's ...*
The following is a list of some phrases that you could dictate to the pupils:
I'm tired.
I'm thirsty.
I'm hungry.
I'm scared.
The dinner's over.
The lesson's over.
There's a farm over there.
The war's over.
The children can refer to the book when writing their suggestions. While they are doing so, walk around the classroom checking that they do not have any problems.
It is a good idea to set a time limit (10 minutes).
Afterwards, ask one pupil to read out a phrase and another to read out his/her respective suggestion.

4. Unusual suggestions

Tell the children to cut their sentences into strips and to separate the red sentences from the blue ones.
Get the pupils to shuffle the strips and to place them on their desks with the text facing downwards.
Then say:
Red sentences on the right.
Blue sentences on the left.
Then ask one pupil to take a strip saying:
(Name), pick up one strip on your right.
Is it red? Ok. Wait a moment.
Then ask another pupil:
(Name), pick up one strip on your left.
Is it blue? Ok. Now wait a moment.
Point to the first pupil and then the second one saying:
Now, you read your sentence and you give a suggestion.
Rarely will the suggestion match the phrase and this will provoke laughter on the part of the class.

Part II - Introduction

Why traditional stories/legends?

Children love listening to stories and being involved during the narration.
This is true for stories in their mother tongue but it is also so for stories told in L2. Obviously these stories must be introduced gradually and backed up by a text that the children already know in L1.
The story must be compatible with the pupils' linguistic level. The pupils will come across vocabulary and structures they already know in different contexts.
But this does not necessarily mean that the text should not be stimulating. With appropriate activities before, during and after the narration, the children will be able to overcome any difficulties relating to new vocabulary or structures. They will be satisfied with their ability to understand the story as a whole.
The stories are presented in order of difficulty, and many forms of the past tense reappear in more than one story, so once the pupils recognize them they will find it easier to understand the other stories.
Each traditional story and legend comes from a different European country, like Peter Pan's friends, and they have been chosen and adapted to suit the linguistic level of the students of this age. Apart from putting the pupils in a position of having to read a narrative text of a certain standard, these stories also help to improve the children's general knowledge.

When to deal with stories?

The six stories and legends are presented in *Unit 11*. However, you can present some of the stories during the course of the previous units. This would enable you to dilute the activities associated with the stories over time and perhaps collaborate with teachers of other subjects to prepare a play and the appropriate costumes, scenery and background music.

Who tells the story?

All the stories are recorded on the cassette. However, if the story is narrated directly to the children the effect is undoubtedly different both in terms of the direct relationship that is established between the narrator and the listener and the increased emotional involvement.
If you narrate the story to the children you can make it all the more realistic by varying your tone of voice, changing your intonation, using mimes and gestures.
You will also be in a position to evaluate whether it is necessary to reformulate a concept with different words to facilitate comprehension; or tell the story more slowly if the pupils find it difficult to keep up with you; or to stop the narration and to encourage the children to guess what is going to happen; or to clarify linguistic problems or cultural references that are unclear.
For all these reasons, we advise **you** to tell the story the first few times.
The audiocassette is a valid aid as a reference for the narration.
Subsequently, you could let the pupils listen to the story on the tape in order to give them the opportunity to hear a *native speaker* narrating the story.

How to listen to stories

As you tell the story the pupils should sit in a semi-circle around you and everybody should be able to see you because your facial expressions and gestures are just as important in conveying the meaning as the use of *flashcards* and illustrations.
The pupils must be encouraged to

participate in the narration in various ways (ref. *while listening activities*).
In this way you will keep them interested and facilitate the learning process.

ACTIVITIES

The following activities provide teaching ideas for all the stories and legends in *Unit 11*. A separate section follows each story with specific follow-up activities.

PRE-LISTENING ACTIVITIES

1. If children know the story in L1 ...
Attract the children's attention by expressing your intention to tell a story in English. Hint at the contents of the story and then ask if any of the children know the story in L1.
If they do, this is a good starting point for a *brainstorming* activity to reconstruct the outline of the story.

2. If children do not know the story in L1 ...
If nobody knows the story, first tell it in L1.
If you wish you could leave the end untold and get the pupils to guess the conclusion. Write the various ideas on the blackboard.
Then tell the story in English, from the beginning to the end, with the help of *flashcards*, as indicated in the *while listening activities*. At the end of the story ask the children whether they have understood the conclusion. Afterwards, check who guessed the correct ending or whether any of the guesses were similar to the real ending.

3. Let's prepare flashcards for key words
Get the pupils to prepare *flashcards* illustrating the key words in the story. Use some of the following *guessing games* to help the students remember the meaning of the words:

a. Show two *flashcards* at a time and say the words asking the pupils to repeat. Make sure the rhythm is quite rapid.
Hold up one flashcard asking:
What is it?
Continue in this way with all the *flashcards*.

b. Show the class three *flashcards*, say the words and ask the pupils to repeat a few times.
Then turn the *flashcards* round and ask, for example:
Where's the (King)?
One pupil has to touch the card and say:
Here!
Pull out the card, show it to the class saying:
Is this the (King)?
The students reply all together with a short answer. Then shuffle the cards saying:
Shuffle, shuffle ... and repeat with another pupil asking him/her to guess where another picture is. Once the children have learnt the words, move on to another set of *flashcards*.

c. Who's got ...?
Divide the class into two groups: A and B. Ask the children in group A to come up to the front of the class and to stand one next to the other.
Give each pupil a *flashcard* and tell them not to show their card to their classmates.
Then say to group A:
Show me your cards.
Say to group B:
Now, look carefully!
After a few moments ask:
Are you ready?
If everybody says they are ready say to group A:
Turn over!
Then ask one child in group B: *Who's got the king?*

The child has to say which student he thinks has got the *flashcard* with that picture. To check ask:
(name), show me your card.
Is that the (king)?
If the child's guess is correct then he/she takes his/her classmate's place and the game starts again. Otherwise, if the guess is wrong, ask another member of group B to give the right answer.

WHILE LISTENING ACTIVITIES

While you read the story you could do one of the following activities:

1. Listen and look
Tell the pupils to listen to the story.
Hold up the illustrations or the *flashcards* when you say the key words during the narration of the story.

2. Listen and show
Hand out the *flashcards* to the corresponding number of pupils and get them to stand next to you.
Each time they hear the word illustrated on their *flashcard* they have to show it to the rest of the class.

3. Look and say
Tell the story, showing the *flashcards* instead of saying the word. The pupils have to say the word all together.

4. Fill in the gap
Prepare a sheet of paper for each member of the class.
Write one word from the text on each sheet of paper, so that all the words are different.
While you are telling the story, replace those words with a *beep*. The child who thinks he/she has got the word to be inserted, holds up the sheet of paper with the word in big letters, saying it out loud.

5. Play a role in the narration
On the blackboard write the phrases that the pupils have to read out during the narration.
When you tell them to do so, the children say the phrases either individually or in groups.

AFTER LISTENING ACTIVITIES

In order to arouse the pupils' interest in the written text the following activities will prove both enjoyable and a good way of practising vocabulary and grammatical structures.
Present these activities in the form of games to be played individually, in pairs or in groups.
Make sure that the pairs or the groups are as homogeneous as possible with regard to linguistic ability.

1. Underline the words you recognize
(individual)
Tell the students to read the text silently and to underline the words they recognize.
Afterwards, get them to count the words and compare the total with the number of words in the text.
The fact that this activity is done after the narration of the story, should enable the children to recognize a certain number of words and to feel satisfied with their ability.
This activity could be done two or three times.
Each time, tell the children to underline the words with a different colour. This will allow you to see how the text has been gradually assimilated.

2. Let's play with words
(individual/in pairs/in groups)
Tell the children to count how many times a particular word appears in the text; to circle opposites, plural forms etc.; to find words that differ only because of a different vowel or consonant, etc.

3. Awareness of the past tenses (individual)
All the stories contain verbs in the past tense which will become part of the students' passive vocabulary. Point out that, like all the stories about events that occurred a long time ago, the narration is in the past tense. Tell the children that the past tense in English comes in two forms, one that is easy to recognize because of the final *-ed* at the end of the verb. Ask the pupils to read the text silently and to circle the verbs that end in *-ed* in red. Read out the list with the correct pronunciation (/t/, /d/, /id/) supplying the equivalent in L1 if necessary.
Afterwards, write the irregular verbs that appear in the text on the blackboard and get the pupils to circle them in blue. Give the children the equivalent in L1 if necessary.
It might prove useful to create a poster with a list of the forms of the past tense that the children come across. This vocabulary can be referred to when reading and understanding other stories. Update the poster as you meet new verb forms.

4. Questions (individual/all together)
There are a series of questions for each story, obviously in the past tense. These questions could be used in the following way:

a. You could write each question on a strip of paper and the respective answers on other strips.
Divide the class into two teams: hand out the questions to one team and give the answers to the other.
Each pupil has to find his/her partner with the matching strip. The pairs give you back the strips of paper.
Check whether the strips have been matched correctly.

b. Keep the questions yourself and distribute the answers (either to individual pupils or pairs).
Read out the questions.
The student with the right answer reads it out and hands you the strip.

c. Read out each question and get the pupils to find the answer by scanning the text. *Yes/No* answers or unstructured answers (that supply the information requested) are sufficient.
It is important that the students understand the question and find the appropriate answer in the text.

5. Reconstructing the text
Photocopy the text. Cut it into different strips so that each one contains one or more sentences. You could suggest the following activities:

a. Each pupil reads his/her strip silently.
Narrate the story pausing briefly at the end of each segment of the text.
The children have to line up one beside the other so that they can reconstruct the story as you tell it.

b. The pupils walk around the classroom freely and try to reconstruct the story.

c. Split the children into groups. Give each group an envelope containing the strips with the different parts of the story.
The first group to put the story together wins the game. If they make a mistake, start the game again and continue until one group manages to reconstruct the original story.

6. Give a title to the story
Get the children to think up a suitable title for the story. Choose the most appropriate title and get the pupils to copy it into their textbooks.

7. Is there a moral in the story?
If the story has a moral discuss it with the children referring to their daily lives.

FOLLOW-UP ACTIVITIES

1. Let's make a book

You could ask the children to illustrate the story on A4 sheets of paper which will then be pinned together to form a book.

2. Let's make a poster

You could make an illustrated poster divided into scenes.

Decide whether to copy out the texts as general reference for the class or to use the poster without the written texts so that the children can tell the story in their own words using the structures they know.

3. Dramatization

You could get the children to act out the story/legend according to the ideas given in the respective section.

Given the limited number of characters in each story, the pupils could dramatize more than one story at a time.

You could narrate the story in L2, or a member of the class could be the narrator, using L1, if the play is to be performed at the end of the year in front of parents or other classes.

A Greek legend: King Midas pages 74-75

This is a Greek legend.
It's the story of a king named Midas.
He was a rich man. He lived in a big palace with lots of gold and silver inside, and a very big garden outside.

He had a daughter. She was nice and sweet.
She spent a lot of time in the garden because she loved flowers.
Everyday she picked roses for her father.

Her father was happy. He loved his gold and silver, and he loved his daughter, too!

But King Midas had a secret wish. One day he asked the gods:

I love gold,
please turn to gold everything I can hold.
I love gold so much,
please turn to gold everything I can touch!

74

And the gods made his wish come true...

Now King Midas was happier than before:
everything he touched turned to gold.

He wanted to kiss his daughter but...
she turned to gold, too!

Poor King Midas! He was desperate and asked the gods:

Please take away all my gold.
My precious daughter is all I want!

Then he kissed his daughter on her nose and she returned to the nice, sweet girl again.

They lived happily in the palace without gold but with lots of love.

75

Materials: *Flashcards* prepared by the children (drawings or pictures glued onto cards) illustrating the following vocabulary: *king, daughter, palace, silver, gold, garden, flowers, roses, gods, to kiss, to hold, to touch.*
Verbs in the past tense: *named, was, lived, had, spent, loved, picked, asked, made, touched, turned, wanted, kissed, returned.*

PRE-LISTENING ACTIVITIES

1. If children know the story in L1 ...

2. If children do not know the story in L1 ...

3. Let's prepare flashcards for key words.

WHILE LISTENING ACTIVITIES

1. Listen and look.

2. Listen and show.

3. Look and say.

4. Fill in the gap.

5. Play a role in the narration
Write the following rhyme on the blackboard:
I love gold,
please turn to gold everything I can hold.
I love gold so much,
please turn to gold everything I can touch.
Please take away my gold.
My precious daughter is all I want.

Get the children to repeat the rhyme a few times all together.
They will take the part of King Midas when the rhyme has to be said.

AFTER LISTENING ACTIVITIES

1. Underline the words you recognize

2. Let's play with words

- Ask the pupils to find out how many times the word *gold* appears (10 times);
- tell the children to link the possessive adjectives *his/her* with the corresponding nouns;
- find two pairs of opposites (*rich/poor, inside/outside*);
- draw a line down the middle of the blackboard: on one side write the heading *King Midas* on the other *the king's daughter*. Beneath each heading the children have to list the adjectives referring to each character.

3. Awareness of the past tenses.

4. Questions

What nationality is this legend?
What's the name of the Greek king?
Was King Midas rich or poor?
Where did the king live?
What was there inside the palace?
What was there outside the palace?
Did the king have a daughter or a son?
What was the king's daughter like?
What did the girl do in the garden?
What did King Midas ask the gods one day?
Did the gods make his wish come true?
What happened then?
What happened when the king wanted to kiss his daughter?
What did King Midas ask the gods?
Where did King Midas kiss his daughter?
Did the king's daughter return to the nice, sweet girl again?
How does the story end?

5. Reconstructing the text.

6. Give a title to the story.

7. Is there a moral in the story?

FOLLOW-UP ACTIVITIES

1. Let's make a book

2. Let's make a poster

3. Dramatization:
Characters: narrator, King Midas, his daughter.

Narrator:	*Characters:*
This is a Greek legend. It's the story of a king named Midas.	*Hello! I'm King Midas. I'm a rich man.* *I live in a big palace with lots of gold and silver inside, and a very big garden outside.*

The King had a daughter. She was nice and sweet.	*Hello! I'm the King's daughter.*
She spent a lot of time in the garden. Everyday she picked roses for her father.	*I love flowers! These roses are beautiful. I'll pick them for my father.*
Her father was happy.	*I love gold and I love silver but ... I love my daughter best of all.*
But King Midas had a secret wish. One day he asked the gods:	*I love gold, please turn to gold everything I can hold. I love gold so much, please turn to gold everything I can touch!*
And the gods made his wish come true... Now King Midas was happier than before: everything he touched turned to gold.	*Hmm. Lovely apples! Oh no, they're... golden apples! Hmm. Lovely bananas! Oh no, they're... golden bananas! Hmm. Lovely bread! Oh no, it's... golden bread! Hmm. Lovely chicken! Oh no, It's... golden chicken! I'm hungry!*
One day he kissed his daughter and... she turned to gold, too!	*Oh, poor me!*
King Midas was desperate and asked the gods:	*Please take away all my gold. My precious daughter is all I want!*
Then he kissed his daughter on her nose and she returned to the nice, sweet girl again	*(They kiss)*
They lived happily in the palace without gold with lots of love.	*I love you, dad. I love you, my dear.*

A Norwegian legend: The three goats - pages 76-77

This is a Norwegian legend.
It's the story of three goats.
They lived in a big green garden full of clover and flowers.
They spent all their time eating clover and flowers but...
... one day there were no more and the three goats were hungry!

Next to the garden there was a bridge to another garden, full of giant clover and colourful flowers.

But the three goats couldn't cross the bridge!

Under the bridge lived a troll. He ate anyone who crossed the bridge.

It was dangerous, but the three goats tried, one at a time.

76

The first goat went over the bridge and told the troll:
Please, don't eat me. I'm only a small goat.
The goat behind me isn't small: it's big. You can eat more!
And the troll waited for the second goat.

The second goat went over the bridge and told the troll:
Please, don't eat me. I'm only a big goat.
The goat behind me is very big and very fat. You can eat more!
And the troll waited for the third goat.

The third goat went over the bridge and told the troll:
I'm very big and very fat.
The troll jumped onto the bridge and the goat kicked the troll off the bridge, far away.

The three goats met again in the garden full of giant clover and colourful flowers.
They're still there now.
They're eating all the clover and all the flowers.

77

Materials: *Flashcards* prepared by the children (drawings or pictures glued onto cards) illustrating the following vocabulary: *small goat, big goat, very big and fat goat, clover, flowers, troll, to kick.*
Verbs in the past tense: *lived, spent, were, was, couldn't cross, ate, crossed, tried, went, told, waited for, jumped, kicked, met.*

PRE-LISTENING ACTIVITIES

1. If children know the story in L1...

2. If children do not know the story in L1...

3. Let's prepare flashcards for key words.

WHILE LISTENING ACTIVITIES

1. Listen and look.

2. Listen and show.

3. Look and say.

4. Fill in the gap.

5. Play a role in the narration.
On the blackboard write what the three goats say:
1 - Please, don't eat me. I'm a small goat.
The goat behind me isn't small: it's big.
You can eat more!
2 - Please, don't eat me. I'm only a big goat.
The goat behind me is very big and very fat.
You can eat more!
3 - I'm very big and very fat!

Get the children to repeat what the goats say a few times until they acquire a fluency of expression. The students will take the part of the goats all together. Otherwise, the class could be divided into three groups giving each one the role of one of the goats.

AFTER LISTENING ACTIVITIES

1. Underline the words you recognize.

2. Let's play with words.

- Tell the children to find the ordinal numbers in the text: *first, second, third*;
- the pupils have to find an adjective in the text which is also the name of a character in a fairy tale (*giant*);
- the students have to underline the prepositions of place:

in, next to, to, under, over, onto, off.

Help the children with the new prepositions if necessary. Get them to draw pictures illustrating the prepositions, preferably with reference to the text.

3. Awareness of the past tenses.

4. Questions.

What nationality is the story of the three goats?
Where did the goats live?
How did the goats spend their time?
What happened one day?
What was there next to the garden?
What was the garden like?
Could the three goats cross the bridge?
Who lived under the bridge?
What did the troll do there?
Did the goats try to cross the bridge despite the dangerous troll?
Who went first?
What did the first goat tell the troll?
What did the troll do?
Who went second?
What did the second goat tell the troll?
What did the troll do?
Who went third?
What did the third goat tell the troll?
What did the troll do?
What did the third goat do then?
Did the three goats meet again?
Where are the three goats now?
What are the three goats doing?

5. Reconstructing the text.

6. Give a title to the story.

7. Is there a moral in the story?

FOLLOW-UP ACTIVITIES

1. Let's make a book

2. Let's make a poster

3. Dramatization:

Characters: narrator, small goat, big goat, very big and very fat goat, troll.

Narrator:	*Characters:*
This is a Norwegian legend. It's the story of three goats.	*- Hello, I'm the small goat.* *- Hello, I'm the big goat.* *- Hello, I'm the very big and very fat goat.*

They lived in a big green garden full of clover and flowers.

- *I like clover. Clover is good.*
- *I like flowers. Flowers are very good.*
- *I like clover and flowers. They are delicious.*

They spent all their time eating clover and flowers but...... one day there were no more and the three goats were hungry.

- *Oh, poor me. No more clover. I'm hungry.*
- *Oh, poor me. No more flowers. I'm very hungry.*
- *Oh, poor me. No more clover. No more flowers. I'm very, very hungry.*

Next to the garden there was a bridge to another garden, full of giant clover and colourful flowers.

Under the bridge lived a troll. *Hello, I'm a troll. I'm dangerous. Watch out!*

He ate anyone who crossed the bridge.

But the three goats tried, one at a time.

The first goat went over the bridge and told the troll: *Please, don't eat me. I'm only a small goat. The goat behind me isn't small: it's big. You can eat more!*

And the troll said: *OK, I'll wait for the second goat.*

The second goat went over the bridge and told the troll: *Please, don't eat me. I'm only a big goat. The goat behind me is very big and very fat. You can eat more!*

And the troll said: *OK, I'll wait for the third goat.*

The third goat went over the bridge and told the troll: *I'm very big and very fat.*

The troll jumped onto the bridge and said: *Now, I'll eat you.*

But the goat kicked the troll off the bridge, far away. *Oihhhhhhhh!*

The three goats met again in the garden full of giant clover and colourful flowers. They're still there now. They're eating all the clover and all the flowers. (all) *Bye-bye.*

A Spanish story: Don Quixote - pages 78-79

This is a Spanish story.
It's the story of Don Quixote.
He was a knight and travelled all around Spain with his servant, Sancho Panza.

Don Quixote was tall and thin and he rode a horse.
His servant Sancho was short and fat and rode a mule.

Don Quixote liked to fight: he saw enemies everywhere.

One day, while they were travelling, Don Quixote told his servant:
Over there, there are some giants! They're our enemies!

Poor Sancho answered:
But sir, they're not giants: they're windmills!

78

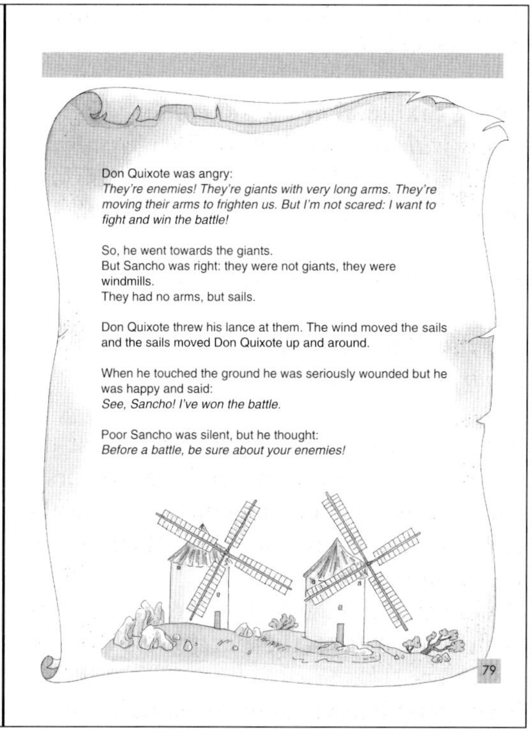

Don Quixote was angry:
They're enemies! They're giants with very long arms. They're moving their arms to frighten us. But I'm not scared: I want to fight and win the battle!

So, he went towards the giants.
But Sancho was right: they were not giants, they were windmills.
They had no arms, but sails.

Don Quixote threw his lance at them. The wind moved the sails and the sails moved Don Quixote up and around.

When he touched the ground he was seriously wounded but he was happy and said:
See, Sancho! I've won the battle.

Poor Sancho was silent, but he thought:
Before a battle, be sure about your enemies!

79

Materials: *Flashcards* prepared by the pupils (drawings or pictures glued onto cards) illustrating the following vocabulary: *knight, servant, horse, mule, giants, windmills.*
Verbs in the past tense: *travelled, was, rode, liked, saw, told, answered, went, had, threw, moved, touched, wounded, thought.*

PRE-LISTENING ACTIVITIES

1. If children know the story in L1...

2. If children do not know the story in L1...

3. Let's prepare flashcards for key words.

WHILE LISTENING ACTIVITIES

1. Listen and look.

2. Listen and show.

3. Look and say.

4. Fill in the gap.

5. Play a role in the narration
Write what the two characters say on the blackboard.
In two groups, the pupils pretend to be Don Quixote and Sancho Panza:

Don Quixote: *Over there, there are some giants! They're our enemies.*

Sancho Panza: *But sir, they're not giants: they're windmills!*

Don Quixote: *They're enemies! They're giants with very long arms. They're moving their arms to frighten us. But I'm not scared: I want to fight and win the battle!*
.....
See Sancho! I've won the battle.

Sancho Panza: *Before a battle, be sure about your enemies!*

It would be a good idea to write what the two characters say in two different colours.
Afterwards, get the students to repeat the dialogue until they can say it fluently and with confidence.
Divide the class into two groups getting each one to take the part of one of the characters.
Each group intervenes in the narration at the right moment.

AFTER LISTENING ACTIVITIES

1. Underline the words you recognize.

2. Let's play with words.

- The pupils have to dictate the physical characteristics of the two characters. Draw two distinct columns on the blackboard and write up what the children say. You could also add other details.

3. Awareness of the past tenses.

4. Questions.
What nationality is this story?
Who was Don Quixote?
What was Don Quixote like?
What did Don Quixote ride?
Who was Sancho Panza?
What was Sancho Panza like?
What did Sancho Panza ride?
What did Don Quixote like to do?
What did Don Quixote tell his servant one day?
What did Sancho answer?
Did Don Quixote fight the "giants"?
Were the "giants" real giants?
What happened when the wind moved the sails?
What did Don Quixote say when he touched the ground?
What did poor Sancho think?

5. Reconstructing the text.

6. Give a title to the story.

7. Is there a moral in the story?

FOLLOW-UP ACTIVITIES

1. Let's make a book

2. Let's make a poster

3. Dramatization:
Characters: narrator, Don Quixote, Sancho Panza

Narrator:	*Characters:*
This is a Spanish story. It's the story of Don Quixote.	*Good morning, my name's Don Quixote and I'm a Spanish knight. As you can see, I'm riding a horse.*
Don Quixote travelled all around Spain with his servant.	*Hello, I'm Sancho Panza and I'm the knight's servant. As you can see, I'm riding a mule.*
Don Quixote liked to fight: he saw enemies everywhere. One day, while they were travelling, Don Quixote told his servant:	*Over there, there are some giants! They're our enemies!*
Poor Sancho answered:	*But sir, they're not giants: they're windmills!*
Don Quixote was angry:	*They're enemies! They're giants with very long arms. They're moving their arms to frighten us. But I'm not scared: I want to fight and win the battle!*
So, he went towards the giants. But Sancho was right: they were not giants, they were windmills. They had no arms, but sails.	
Don Quixote threw his lance at them.	*I'll kill you!*
The wind moved the sails and the sails moved Don Quixote up and around.	(in the distance) *Oih! Oih! Help, help!*
When Don Quixote touched the ground he was seriously wounded but he was happy and said:	*See, Sancho! I've won the battle.*
Poor Sancho was silent, but he thought:	*Before a battle, be sure about your enemies!*

A German legend: The River Rhine - pages 80-81

This is a German legend.
It's the story of a very big river: the River Rhine.
It is so big that once it was considered the Father of Germany.
The river was shining and bright.
There was gold hidden inside it.

The Ondines lived in the river.
Everyday they played and looked after the gold.

But one day, the gold was stolen by the gods and the River Rhine became dark!

The Ondines cried and asked the gods:
Please give the gold back to the Rhine!

80

But the gods wanted the gold for themselves.
They built a golden palace where they lived happily.

The Ondines cried and cried and asked the Sun for help:
Please Sun, shine into the river and make the Rhine bright again!
But the Sun couldn't help them.

At last, the Rhine heard their cries. He raised his waves high up in the sky and took back his gold and the golden palace, too.

The River Rhine became brighter than before and the Ondines lived happily ever after.

81

Materials: *Flashcards* (with drawings or pictures glued onto cards) illustrating the following vocabulary: *river, gold, the Ondines, gods, golden palace, sun, waves.*
Verbs in the past tense: *considered, was, lived, played, looked after, stolen, became, cried, asked, wanted, built, couldn't help, heard, raised, took back.*

PRE-LISTENING ACTIVITIES

1. If children know the story in L1...

2. If children do not know the story in L1...

3. Let's prepare flashcards for key words.

WHILE LISTENING ACTIVITIES

1. Listen and look.

2. Listen and show.

3. Look and say.

4. Fill in the gap.

5. Play a role in the narration.
Write what the Ondines say on the blackboard. The children will have to repeat the words all together:

- *Please give the gold back to the Rhine!*
- *Please Sun, shine into the river and make the Rhine bright again!*

AFTER LISTENING ACTIVITIES

1. Underline the words you recognize.

2. Let's play with words.

- Tell the children to underline the adjectives that refer to the river. Which is the longest adjective?
- The children have to count how many times the word *gods* appears. (3)

3. Awareness of the past tenses.

4. Questions.

What nationality is this legend?
What's the name of the river?
What was the river like?
What was hidden inside the river?
Who lived in the river?
What did the Ondines do every day?
What happened one day?
What was the River Rhine like?
What did the Ondines ask the gods?
Did the gods give the gold back to the Rhine?
What did the gods build?
Did the Sun help the Ondines?
Who helped the Ondines in the end?
What did the River Rhine do?
How does the story end?

5. Reconstructing the text.

6. Give a title to the story.

7. Is there a moral in the story?

FOLLOW-UP ACTIVITIES

1. Let's make a book

2. Let's make a poster

3. Dramatization

Characters: narrator, River Rhine, Ondines, gods, Sun.

Narrator:	*Characters:*
This is a German legend. It's the story of a very big river: the River Rhine.	*Hello, I'm the River Rhine. I'm a very big river in Germany. That's why I'm called the Father of Germany.*
The river was shining and bright. There was gold hidden inside it.	
The Ondines lived in the river.	*Hello, we are the Ondines. We look after the gold and we play all day in the river.*

But one day, the gold was stolen by the gods and the River Rhine became dark. *Oh, poor me! Where's my gold? Where's my gold?*

The Ondines cried and asked the gods: *Please give the gold back to the Rhine!*

But the gods wanted the gold for themselves. *No, never!*

They built a golden palace where they lived happily.

The Ondines cried and cried and asked the Sun for help: *Please Sun, shine into the river and make the Rhine bright again!*

But the Sun couldn't help them. *I'm sorry I can't.*

At last, the Rhine heard their cries and said: *Don't worry. I'll help you.*

He raised his waves high up in the sky and took back his gold and the golden palace, too. *At last, I've got my gold back again.*

The River Rhine became brighter than before and the Ondines lived happily ever after.

A British legend: King Arthur - pages 82-83

This is a British legend.
It's the story of little Arthur who then became a very famous king.

Some time before Arthur's birth, his father fell ill. He called his magician Merlin and asked him to cure his illness.
The magician cured the king but, in return, asked him for his first child.

When the child was born, the magician came and asked for the baby whose name was Arthur.
Merlin took him to Sir Ector's castle where Arthur lived happily with his elder stepbrother Kay.

Time passed and the king died leaving no heir.
People wondered: *Who will be king now?*

82

On Christmas day, in front of the church, an anvil appeared, and in it there was a sword.
In front of the anvil there was a message:
He who pulls the sword out of the anvil will become king.
Many people tried but nobody succeeded.

On 1st January there was a tournament, and Kay asked Arthur to go and fetch his sword from the castle.

Arthur went there but he didn't find the sword so he came back. While he was passing in front of the church he saw the sword in the anvil and thought: *I'll take this one.*
He pulled the sword out of the anvil and took it to his stepbrother.

When people saw him with the sword, they called him, king Arthur.

King Arthur called the sword Excalibur.

83

Materials: *Flashcards* (with drawings or pictures glued onto cards) illustrating the following vocabulary: *king, magician, baby, stepbrother, anvil, sword, people.*
Verbs in the past tense: *became, fell ill, called, asked, cured, was, came, took, lived, passed, died, wondered, appeared, tried, succeeded, went, saw, thought, pulled.*

PRE-LISTENING ACTIVITIES

1. If children know the story in L1...

2. If children do not know the story in L1...

3. Let's prepare flashcards for key words.

WHILE LISTENING ACTIVITIES

1. Listen and look.

2. Listen and show.

3. Look and say.

4. Fill in the gap.

5. Play a role in the narration.
Divide the class into three groups and each one will take one of the following parts:
- the people: *Who will be king now?*
- voice reading out the message: *He who pulls the sword out of the anvil will become king.*
- Arthur: *I'll take this one.*

AFTER LISTENING ACTIVITIES

1. Underline the words you recognize.

2. Let's play with words.
- Ask the children to count how many times the word *king* appears in the text and to say who it refers to;
- the children have to discover which word can be obtained from *sword* after moving one consonant (*words*);
- the children have to find out which word can be obtained from *heir* by changing one vowel (*hair*).

3. Awareness of the past tenses.

4. Questions.
Who was Arthur?
What happened before Arthur's birth?
What did the king ask his magician Merlin?
What did the magician ask in return?
What was the baby's name?
Where did Merlin take Arthur?
What was the name of his stepbrother?
What did people wonder when the king died leaving no heir?
What appeared in front of the church on Christmas day?
What was there in the anvil?
What did the message on the anvil say?
What happened the day of the tournament?
Did Arthur find the sword?
What did Arthur think when he saw the sword in the anvil?
What did the people say when they saw Arthur with the sword?
What did King Arthur call the sword?

5. Reconstructing the text.

6. Give a title to the story.

7. Is there a moral in the story?

FOLLOW-UP ACTIVITIES

1. Let's make a book

2. Let's make a poster

3. Dramatization:
Characters: narrator, king, magician Merlin, Arthur, Kay, people.

Narrator:	*Characters:*
This is a British legend. It's the story of little Arthur who then became a very famous king.	
Some time before Arthur's birth, his father fell ill.	*Oh, I feel so ill. I need magician Merlin. He can cure my illness.*

The magician cured the king but,
in return, asked for his first child.

This magic potion is for you, but first promise that, in return, I'll have your first child.

The king was desperate but he agreed.

I promise.

When the child was born, the magician came
and asked for the baby whose name was Arthur.

I know a baby boy is born.
Please, give him to me.

Merlin took Arthur to Sir Hector's castle where
he lived happily with his elder stepbrother Kay.

Time passed and the king died leaving no heir.
People wondered:

Who will be king now?

On Christmas day, in front of the church,
an anvil appeared and in it there was a sword.

The people passing by were very surprised:
(three people comment)

- *What's that?*
- *A sword!*
- *A sword in an anvil?*

In front of the anvil there was a message:

He who pulls the sword out of the anvil will become king.

Many people tried but nobody succeeded.
(three people step forward)

- *I'll try first.*
- *I'll go next.*
- *Then it will be my turn.*

On 1st January there was a tournament.

Kay: *Please, go and fetch my sword.*
Arthur: *Where is it?*
Kay: *In my bedroom, in the castle.*

Arthur went there but he didn't find
the sword so he came back.
While he was passing in front
of the church he saw the sword
in the anvil and thought:

I'll take this one.

He pulled the sword out of the anvil and
took it to his stepfather. But when people
saw him with the sword, they said:

Here is our king, our King Arthur.
Hurray, hurray!

King Arthur called the sword Excalibur.

A French legend: Orlando's madness - pages 84-85

This is a French legend.
It's the story of a knight named Orlando.
He was the nephew of Charlemagne.
Orlando fought and won many battles: he was considered a great hero.

But he was strong in battle and weak in heart.
In fact, he went mad for love.
He was in love with Angelica, but she didn't love him.

That's why he went mad: poor Orlando!

But Astolfo cured him of his madness.
Astolfo was a hero, too.
After many battles, he decided to take a trip to the moon riding his winged horse.

84

Once on the moon, he noticed some little bottles and asked:
What are they for?

The answer was:
Men on earth sometimes lose their reason and go mad.
As you can see, on each bottle there's a name: it's the name of a mad man and inside there's his reason.

Astolfo looked for the bottle with Orlando's name.
He found it and brought it back to his friend Orlando.

Orlando became a great hero again and carried on his heroic battles.

85

Materials: *Flashcards* (with drawings or pictures glued onto cards) illustrating the following vocabulary: *knight, moon, winged horse, bottles.*
Verbs in the past tense: *named, fought, won, considered, went mad, cured, decided, noticed, asked, looked for, found, brought, became, carried on.*

PRE-LISTENING ACTIVITIES

1. If children know the story in L1...

2. If children do not know the story in L1...

3. Let's prepare flashcards for key words.

WHILE LISTENING ACTIVITIES

1. Listen and look.

2. Listen and show.

3. Look and say.

4. Fill in the gap.

5. Play a role in the narration.
On the blackboard write what Astolfo finds on the moon with reference to the contents of the bottles:

Men on earth sometimes lose their reason and go mad.
As you can see, on each bottle there's a name: it's the name of a mad man and inside there's his reason.

The pupils read out this part all together to acquire fluency.
They will take part in the narration at the appropriate moment.

AFTER LISTENING ACTIVITIES

1. Underline the words you recognize.

2. Let's play with words.
- Tell the students to discover what word they can obtain from *bottle* by changing only one vowel (*battle*);
- the children have to count how many times the word *hero* appears and to find its corresponding adjective (*heroic*).

3. Awareness of the past tenses.

4. Questions
What nationality is this legend?
What was the knight's name?
Was Orlando a great hero?
Did Orlando love Angelica?
Did Angelica love Orlando?
What happened to Orlando?
Who cured Orlando of his madness?
What did Astolfo do?
What did Astolfo notice on the moon?
What was there on each bottle?
What was there inside each bottle?
Did Astolfo find the bottle with Orlando's name?
Did Orlando drink from the bottle?
What happened then?

5. Reconstructing the text.

6. Give a title to the story.

7. Is there a moral in the story?

FOLLOW-UP ACTIVITIES

1. Let's make a book

2. Let's make a poster

3. Dramatization:
Characters: narrator, Orlando, Astolfo, voice on the moon.

Narrator:	*Characters:*
This is a French legend. It's the story of a knight named Orlando.	 *Hello, my name's Orlando. I'm a French knight.* *I'm the nephew of Charlemagne,* *the King of France.*
Orlando fought and won many battles: he was considered a great hero.	
But he was strong in battle and weak in heart. In fact, he went mad for love.	 *I'm in love with Angelica.*

I love her beautiful eyes,
I love her beautiful long hair...
her arms, her hands.. but there's a problem.
She doesn't love me. Oh, poor me.
What can I do? What can I do?

That's why he went mad: poor Orlando.

Fortunately, Orlando had a very good friend: *Hello, I'm Astolfo.*
I'm Orlando's best friend.
He is so desperate. What can I do to help him?

Astolfo was a hero, too.
After many battles, he decided to take
a trip to the moon riding his winged horse.

Once on the moon, he noticed some
little bottles and asked: *What are they for?*

The answer was: *Men on earth sometimes lose their reason and go mad. As you can see, on each bottle there's a name: it's the name of a mad man and inside there's his reason.*

Astolfo looked for the bottle
with Orlando's name: *Rupert, Edward, Orlando... Here it is!*

Astolfo took the bottle and brought it back
to his friend Orlando. *Orlando, my dear friend. Drink this!*

Thanks to his friend Astolfo, Orlando
became a great hero again and carried
on his heroic battles.

CONCLUSION

1. Think and answer (p. 86-87)
As a final activity, once the stories and legends have been read in *Unit 11* get the children to do the multiple choice exercise on pages 86 and 87. The pupils have to choose the answers on the basis of what they can remember without consulting their textbooks.
The exercise could be done either individually, in pairs or in groups.
(Solutions: 1b, 2a, 3c, 4c, 5a, 6c, 7b, 8c, 9a).
Ask the children to answer the tenth question by expressing their choice orally.

Unit 12 - A new adventure

Lesson 1 pages 88-89

Vocabulary: *legends, miss, not much, free, friendship, adventures, mystery, better than, stay, forever*

I. PRESENTATION: A new adventure

1. Silent reading

Tell the children to read the text silently and then ask whether they have understood what is happening.

If the children know the story of Peter Pan they will be able to understand that the characters, being called by Tinker Bell, leave for another adventure.

2. Look and listen

Get the children to listen to the dialogue as they follow the text in their books.

3. Time for play back

The pupils pretend to be the characters in the story by moving their lips without producing any sounds while they follow the text in their books.

Afterwards, check that everybody has understood all the dialogue.

II. TIME FOR A COMPETITION!

During the last lesson tell the children that they are going to compete in a singing contest. Ask some volunteers to come up to the front of the class either as soloists or in groups.

Each one has to sing one of the nine songs presented in *Magic! 2*.

The remaining pupils form the jury which has evaluate each song on the basis of its

presentation, with a score from 1 to 10.
Give your own evaluation of the pronunciation. The children could use the musical background on the cassette.
The individual or group with the highest score wins the contest.
The competition could also be based on the dramatization of the stories and legends.
Different groups could choose to act out a story as it is presented in the book or they could elaborate the story with creative and more personal variations.
Such a performance could also form part of an end of year play for parents or other classes in the school.

Therefore, you will end the year in an enjoyable way in the company of Peter Pan and his friends.
The adventure is not over. See you next year!

UNIT	FUNCTIONS	STRUCTURES	VOCABULARY
Welcome unit	- Revision of the functions learnt during the previous academic year.	- *Revision of the structures introduced during the previous academic year.*	*Fantastic!, Wonderful!, At last!, island, wood, mountain, lake, volcano, river, sea, village, map.*
1 **Back to Neverland**	- Introducing yourself - Introducing somebody else - Giving a physical description of yourself	- *I am ...* - *These are my friends* - *I'm ... and ... I've got ...*	*Tall, thin, short, fat, eyes, hair, fingers, toes, ears, nose, arms, legs, hands, feet, mouth, yourself, all.*
2 **Peter's family**	- Asking and giving information about your state of health - Asking and saying where somebody comes from and their nationality	- *How are you? Fine thanks* - *What about you?* - *Where are you from? I'm from ...* - *Are you Spanish? Yes, I am / No, I'm not.*	*Great Britain, Greece, Germany, France, Norway, Spain, Italy, brother, sisters, without, German, French, Spanish, Greek, British, Norwegian, Italian.*
3 **Hook is back**	- Asking about somebody's identity - Asking what somebody looks like - Describing somebody in the third person singular - Expressing your state of mind - Recognizing parts of the body	- *Who's ... ?* - *What is he/she like?* - *He/She's ... and ...* - *He/She's got ...* - *I'm happy / sad*	*Pirate, terrible, long, moustache, only, beard, round, happy, sad, surprised, tired, angry, scared, head, shoulders, knees, feet.*
4 **Peter's house**	- Giving orders in the affermative and negative imperative - Asking about possession - Answering affermatively and negatively - Revision of the prepositions of place - Recognizing objects and rooms in a house	- *Let's go! Come on! Come up! Don't be afraid!* - *Have you got ...?* - *Yes, I have / No, I haven't*	*Far, up there, tree house, ladder, washbasin, chair, mirror, sofa, table, wardrobe, fridge, bath, cupboard, television, lamp, bed.*
5 **Going shopping**	- Expressing need and necessity - Describing actions taking place at the moment of speaking - Recognizing shops	- *What do you need? I need ...* - *What are you doing? I'm eating! What is he/she doing?*	*To buy, something, everything, funny, a pair of ..., baker's, greengrocer's, chemist, shoe shop, record shop, clothes shop, pet shop, book shop, toy shop, bread, toothpaste, toothbrush.*

UNIT	FUNCTIONS	STRUCTURES	VOCABULARY
6 **Magic in Neverland**	- Asking about and expressing ability - Recognizing plural demonstrative pronouns - Recognizing wild and domestic animals	- *I can ...* - *Can you ... ?* *Yes, I can / No, I can't* - *These ...* *Those ...*	*Elephant, crocodiles, lions, hippos, sheep, horse, cow, dog, duck, hen, chicks, cat, fly, sing, jump, dance, dangerous, magic.*
7 **Hook's near!**	- Identifying the owner of an object - Distinguishing between left and right	- *Whose ... is that / this?* - *Whose ... are those / these?* - *Right / left*	*Hat, footprints, into, between, watch out!*
8 **The mystery's solved!**	- Recognizing possessive adjectives in the third person singular - Describing somebody's clothing - Identifying clothing on the basis of the parts of the body - Recognizing articles of clothing	- *His / Her* - *What is he/she wearing?* - *What can you put on your (feet)?*	*Clothes, trousers, gloves, T-shirt, shirt, shoes, belt, socks, jacket, blouse, skirt.*
9 **War is over!**	- Expressing ability and inability - Offering help - Understanding and carrying out commands	- *Can you ... ?* *I can / I can't* - *Do you need any help?*	*Swim, hurry up, tricks, no more, war, don't forget, I give up, do magic, climb trees, skate, ride a bicycle, snap fingers, move toes, shake head, wink an eye.*
10 **Another trick!**	- Offering food - Accepting, refusing and expressing a preference - Expressing hunger or thirst - Recognizing food and using the suitable partitive	- *Would you like a/an/some ... ?* - *Yes, please / No thanks* - *I prefer ...*	*Cheers!, dinner, chicken, a piece of cake, biscuits, carrots, apple, plates, bowl, coke, milk, orange juice, lemonade, fruit, cheese, chocolate.*
11 **Stories around the fire**	- Inviting somebody to do something - Listening to and understanding a written text - Recognizing verbs in the past tense	- *What do we do now?* - *Would you like to ... ?* - *What about ... ?*	*Given the quantity of structures and new words in the stories, the vocabulary is listed in the textbook.*